TENNIS
Practice Games

Joe Dinoffer

HUMAN KINETICS

Library of Congress Cataloging-in-Publication Data

Dinoffer, Joe, 1953-
    Tennis practice games / Joe Dinoffer.
       p.   cm.
    ISBN 0-7360-4414-0 (softcover)
  1. Tennis. I. Title.
    GV995 .D627 2003
    796.342--dc21
                                                              2002013212

ISBN: 0-7360-4414-0

Acquisitions Editor: Martin Barnard; **Managing Editor:** Wendy McLaughlin; **Assistant Editor:** Kim Thoren; **Copyeditor:** Jan Feeney; **Proofreader:** Myla Smith; **Permission Manager:** Toni Harte; **Graphic Designer:** Robert Reuther; **Graphic Artist and Illustrator:** Francine Hamerski; **Art and Photo Manager:** Dan Wendt; **Cover Designer:** Keith Blomberg; **Photographer (cover):** Tom Roberts; **Photographer (interior):** © Human Kinetics; **Printer:** United Graphics

Human Kinetics books are available at special discounts for bulk purchase. Special editions or book excerpts can also be created to specification. For details, contact the Special Sales Manager at Human Kinetics.

Printed in the United States

10 9 8 7 6 5 4 3 2 1

Human Kinetics
Web site: http://www.HumanKinetics.com/

United States: Human Kinetics
P.O. Box 5076
Champaign, IL 61825-5076
800-747-4457
e-mail: humank@hkusa.com

Canada: Human Kinetics
475 Devonshire Road Unit 100
Windsor, ON N8Y 2L5
800-465-7301 (in Canada only)
e-mail: orders@hkcanada.com

Europe: Human Kinetics
107 Bradford Road
Stanningley
Leeds LS28 6AT, United Kingdom
+44 (0) 113 255 5665
e-mail: hk@hkeurope.com

Australia: Human Kinetics
57A Price Avenue
Lower Mitcham, South Australia 5062
08 8277 1555
e-mail: liahka@senet.com.au

New Zealand: Human Kinetics
P.O. Box 105-231, Auckland Central
09-523-3462
e-mail: hkp@ihug.co.nz

TENNIS
Practice Games

Contents

PART 2 **Training and Match Strategy** **107**

Preface

Let's begin by agreeing that tennis is the best lifelong sport in the world: It offers more health benefits and social, developmental, and competitive opportunities than any other activity. At the same time, we have to admit that tennis faces at least one significant challenge: Every tennis court I've played on looks the same. Those 490 feet of lines are always in the same place.

I've traveled to more than 50 countries conducting tennis clinics and workshops for nearly 30 years, and I've seen the results of many practice sessions: They can become boring because they are so repetitive. How popular would snow skiing be if every slope on every mountain were identical? How many people would play golf if every single hole were a flat rectangle of the same size and shape? Boring.

Of course, on a tennis court, people solve the problem of repetitiveness by interacting competitively. They get out to play, hit a couple of balls to warm up, and say, "Okay, serve 'em up." But don't get me wrong. Playing a couple of sets every time you go out to play is fine, but how much will that improve your game? Because the satisfaction of improving is one of the top three reasons people play tennis. Of the players I've interviewed, 90 percent play tennis for fun, fitness, *and* the satisfaction of improving.

The drills and games in this book help satisfy all three of these player desires. Don't think of these as simply ideas for practice sessions. They are really much more when considered in the perspective of game-based drilling. When practice is game-based it creates more fun, focus, and fitness, leading to faster improvement than traditional repetitive drilling.

The game and drill variations presented here are proven winners and can be expanded into thousands more. A little imagination is all you need to adapt any of the games to almost any given on-court situation.

I hope you have as much fun trying out these games as I had in compiling them. Remember that tennis is, after all, a game. And every time you walk on the court, you should feel like a child trying out a new toy just received on a birthday.

Acknowledgments

First and foremost I want to express my gratitude and appreciation to the best copyeditor and proofreader in the world, a person who worked long hours on the first draft of the manuscript for this book. When it was submitted to Human Kinetics, we were told it was among the cleanest manuscripts they had ever received. This dedicated and committed copyeditor happens to be my wife of 21 years, Monika Dinoffer.

I also want to express thanks and appreciation to Martin Barnard of Human Kinetics for both his commitment to quality and outstanding attitude. Martin convinced me to work on this project and consistently cleared the path for smooth sailing. In many ways Wendy McLaughlin was the first mate on the journey. As the book's editor, she was nothing short of a pleasure to work with, both competent and encouraging every step of the way.

Finally, I want to thank my parents, who made daily sport possible for me as a child, a pattern I have been fortunate to continue throughout my life. And, finally, to our precious nine-year-old daughter, Kalindi, who keeps me constantly in touch with fun and games by allowing me to see life through the eyes of a child. I don't think this book of games would have been possible without having this little girl in our lives.

Introduction
Game-Based Practice

Sports are broken down into two main categories: closed and open, distinguished by interaction between competitors. Closed sports include golf, swimming, gymnastics, figure skating, bowling, and horseshoes. Open sports include tennis, football, basketball, baseball, and soccer. Interaction creates unlimited variables that force fast decision making and response. Because tennis is an open sport, players should practice, as much as possible, under gamelike conditions.

Tennis has been taught in a very methodical manner. In your first lesson, you started off with forehand groundstrokes, and then moved on to backhands, volleys, and so on. Down the road, you learned how to serve. All this time, you never played a single game and probably didn't even know how to keep score. Yet isn't playing a game the reason you took up tennis in the first place? You bet it is. In fact, many tennis industry insiders attribute a significant part of the drop-off in tennis participation after the boom of the 1970s to just this situation. People took up the game to play it, signed up for lessons, but didn't really get to play—at least not quickly enough.

This traditional way of teaching tennis is why coaches hear players complain, "I played horribly and just can't understand it. In the lesson I was hitting my forehand just fine." What happens is that players prepare for matches with too much stroke repetition without creating a gamelike environment during their practice sessions. Then, in the random environment of a real match, their skills are challenged in a totally different way. Players are simply not prepared. Their strokes naturally break down, and they get frustrated and nervous. The more nervous they become, the more their strokes fall apart. It's a vicious cycle that is very difficult to break in the middle of a match.

Game-based learning reverses the traditional learning sequence found in most sports instruction, which has been based on how academics are often taught in schools. Typically, a teacher gives the information Monday through Thursday, then on Friday quizzes the students by asking questions.

This is called a *directed learning* environment—a one-way street. The teacher teaches (gives information or answers), and the students are supposed to listen like sponges and absorb as much as possible.

The opposite of the traditional directed learning paradigm is game-based learning. Let the players play because, after all, tennis is a game. Through playing, they discover exactly which parts of their games need attention and practice. Then they see the purpose behind practicing and are much more motivated.

Compare it to a child in school who is given an assignment of doing research in the library. Typically, the child begrudgingly goes to the library and clearly does not enjoy the process. It's too much like work. The opposite would be the student who selects her own topic and, out of natural interest and curiosity, goes to the library under her own motivational steam, without being forced to go by the instructor. Which visit to the library will result in greater learning and retention? Studies show that players who discover their own needs are much more motivated to improve and work on their short-comings than others who are simply told what they need to improve.

I am reminded of Swedish superstar Bjorn Borg. As a child, he played against a wall for hours and hours. At first he had no instruction, no coaching at all. Although backboard practice is viewed as repetitive, Borg created games and challenges to keep himself focused, enthusiastic, and entertained. The key ingredient to his success was that he was incredibly motivated by his love for the game. In fact, if his mother had to punish him, she found the most effective punishment was to take away his tennis racket. He was that much in love with the game.

The conclusion? Play the game and have fun. Minimize dead-ball drilling, which is simply bouncing and hitting one ball after another. As far as possible, integrate realistic game situations into all your practice sessions. This includes pausing between points to refocus and prepare for the next point, and it includes changing sides with a small rest every five to ten minutes as well. Simulate real match performance in practice and your real match performance will improve automatically. Any weaknesses that need extra attention (remember that no one's perfect!) will become crystal clear.

Drill Finder

Key

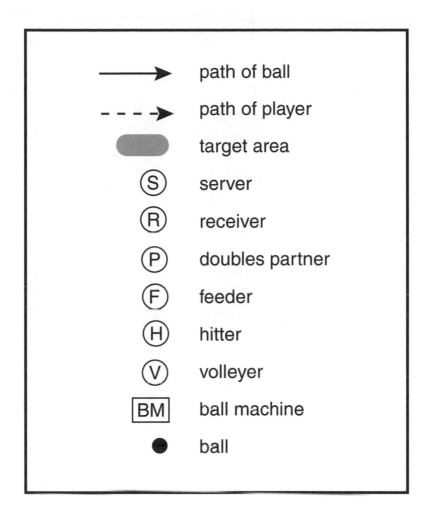

path of ball

path of player

target area

(S) server

(R) receiver

(P) doubles partner

(F) feeder

(H) hitter

(V) volleyer

BM ball machine

● ball

Shotmaking

Laserlike Ball Control

We speak about the importance of the fundamentals of tennis for all levels of play, the foundation on which a successful game is built. For decades, tennis teachers approached each lesson in a conventional fashion with little, if any, room for deviation. At the extreme, a tennis lesson would resemble a dancing lesson with the instructor painting footprints on the dance floor. Each step had to land on an exact spot. In fact, I even know of some tennis instructors who went so far as to paint footprints (or tennis shoe prints) on the courts! Grips and backswings more often than not were taught with the same dogmatic approach as footwork. Shadow swinging as a means to practice and develop technique was commonplace.

Then Bjorn Borg came on the scene with his (at that time extreme) topspin forehand and his two-handed backhand, and many of the tremendous conventions came crashing down. Borg even frequently used open-stance footwork, practically unheard of before his time.

What we've learned from Borg and many since is that the most important fundamental is consistency, which comes from balance and racket control. We have also learned that there are many acceptable ways to get to a tennis ball and hit it.

When you think of laserlike ball control, players like Australia's Lleyton Hewitt come to mind. At every level of play, ball control is an essential part of playing winning tennis.

This chapter consists of games and exercises for building this universal fundamental of solid tennis. Some of the drills in this chapter will also incorporate the principle of "checkpoints," or physical reminders that create consistent strokes. These checkpoints work as tools in a toolbox: Use a specific checkpoint when a certain shot becomes difficult to control or falls apart completely. However, keep in mind that most of these checkpoints will work for most players, but each cannot possibly work for everyone. Therefore, if you understand the principle of checkpoints, you will be able to adapt the exercises for your own style of play.

Finally, in this chapter, you will notice that the drills are oriented more toward cooperating with a partner rather than for competition. So, as you try out some of these exercises, remember that patience is more important than power, and the satisfaction of consistency is more important than receiving occasional praise after hitting an occasional blazing winner.

Racket Circles

1

Description

This exercise is a variation of the ever-popular game of minitennis designed to help players develop quick and agile hands. You and your partner need to start on the service lines and hit a ball cooperatively back and forth with one bounce within the service boxes. Then, to develop quick hands and increase ball control, pass your own rackets in a full circle around your bodies in between hitting each ball.

Helpful Tips

1. Try to use both right and left hands equally when passing the racket around your body.
2. Remember that the nondominant hand actively performs three tasks for every shot: It sets the racket angle and therefore the correct grip, relaxes the racket hand, and helps prepare the racket position for the proper backswing.

Variations

1. As you advance, try this same exercise from the baseline.
2. For an even greater challenge, try it with two racket circles in between every shot.
3. Also try these variations from the volley position where you have even less time.

Soft Hands

Description

This exercise is a creative warm-up drill to help players develop the soft hands needed for successful tennis. Put one, two, or three balls on a partner's racket and stand a few feet away with your racket ready. Have your partner softly toss all the balls from his racket at the same time. Your job is to attempt to supercatch as many of the balls as possible on your own racket. (A supercatch is to quickly maneuver your racket to catch a ball smoothly on the strings without letting it bounce or make a sound.)

Helpful Tips

1. This exercise may seem difficult at first. Start with one ball and a very soft toss and move up from there.

2. You may also want to try self-tossing one ball at a time at first to get a feel for the skill required. If it is difficult, be patient. With some practice, you can master supercatching in a relatively short time.

Variations

1. Begin with one or more balls on your racket; then have your partner softly toss additional balls, one at a time. The goal is to catch the additional balls without dropping the other ball(s) already on your racket.

2. An advanced single-ball supercatch is with one player hitting a groundstroke while the other player is at the net. Instead of volleying the ball back, try catching it on the strings without letting the ball bounce off the racket. Try a few of these and you'll see for yourself how challenging it is.

Strategy

The supercatch is one of those skills that can help a tennis player's overall expertise, even though it is not a specific shot that is required (or legal) on a tennis court. But, touch and soft hands are needed for drop shots and drop volleys. And, on the most advanced levels, think of the soft hands needed to disguise a drop shot when looking as if you are hitting an approach shot. It is even more difficult to occasionally hit a drop shot when returning a second serve.

Pencil Handicap

Description

This drill is sure to add fun and variety, as well as a solid learning opportunity, to any workout. Simply bring a pencil to the court, put it behind your ear, and have your partner do the same. The rules are simple: If the pencil falls out anytime before the end of the point, that player loses the point.

Helpful Tips

1. Keep in mind that this drill is designed to prove a simple point: The more you run your opponent around the court, the more frequently she will lose balance and therefore make errors.

2. When trying this drill, consider how track stars look when they run. Their heads are always level.

Variations

1. This exercise works as a handicapping system as well. With two mismatched players, just give the stronger player the pencil, and anytime the pencil falls, the point is awarded to the weaker player.

2. You can also try this exercise with four people playing doubles.

3. Instead of putting a pencil behind your ear, you can put a tennis cap on your head, upside down. A level head while you're running is a good indicator of overall good balance.

Did you know?

At the pro level, players must change direction an average of seven times per point. This fact amplifies the challenge and importance of being on balance while moving.

Description

This is a terrific warm-up drill that emphasizes ball control. This game is 100% cooperative, but it also encourages a great deal of fast footwork and good recovery skills. In a minitennis setup, place an extra ball on the ground on each of the four back corners of the playing area. To begin, rally with a partner only in one service box with one ball on the ground on each side (on the side T and the center T). In between hits, pick up one of the balls from the court and then place it down on the court again after the next hit. In other words, on one hit the ball is in your hand and on the next hit the ball is on the court.

Helpful Tips

1. Remember that the key to success with this exercise is to recover quickly to either pick up a ball or put it down. If you feel rushed, just hit the ball in play higher over the net to slow things down.

2. After this drill, be sure to play normally. You will feel as if you have all the time in the world.

Variations

1. Play this game cooperatively at first (that is, see if you and your partner can hit 10 or 20 balls in a row). Then, try it competitively: The first player to reach 5 points wins the game.

2. Once you master the game in two boxes, try the same exercise in all four service boxes with two players (see diagram). Cooperatively this will be manageable, but competitively it will probably be too difficult unless the height of the net is raised to force the ball into a higher arc.

3. With four players, have both players on each side of the net pick up and then put down a ball regardless of who hit it. You can also play this variation cooperatively and competitively.

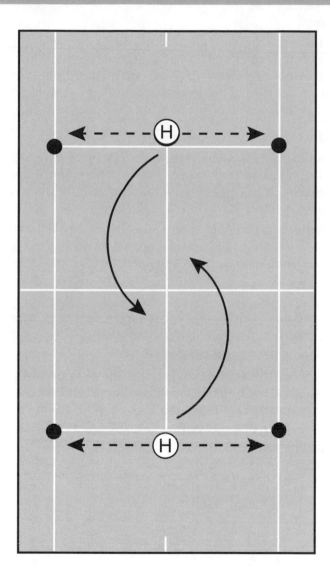

Recovery Groundstrokes

Description

This exercise takes the previous game to the next logical level. If you and your partner were able to control the ball cooperatively within the service boxes, perform the same cooperative exercise from the baseline, at first in just half the singles court. Set a reasonable goal at first (for example, hit 10 balls in a row and either pick up a ball or place it back down after hitting every shot).

Helpful Tips

1. You'll find that you have more time to pick up and place the balls after every shot, compared to the last drill. However, controlling the ball will be more difficult because you will automatically have more court to cover. Keep in mind that control is the key.

2. Focus as much as possible on quick recovery immediately after hitting each ball. If you stand and watch your shot without moving, you'll find yourself in trouble before you know it.

Variations

1. Perform the same drill but this time crosscourt only, from deuce court to deuce court.

2. Go crosscourt from the ad side.

3. After mastering this exercise in half the singles court both down the line and crosscourt, try it in the full singles court, both cooperatively and then competitively (see diagram).

4. For the biggest challenge, try this same idea with one person at the net hitting volleys and the other hitting groundstrokes.

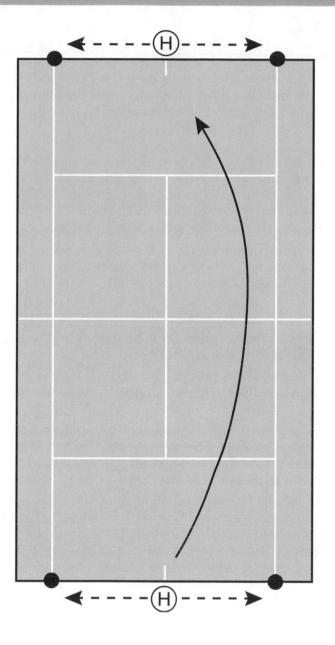

6 360-Degree Groundstrokes

Description

This exercise is designed to help rigid players who don't adequately use their entire bodies to rotate into their shots. If you are one of those players, simply hit a shot and then rotate 360 degrees before the next shot by turning in a complete circle in the same direction in which you are following through. As a result, you should gain a more efficient stroke; you will be able to hit more powerfully with a slower, more effortless swing.

Helpful Tips

1. When performing this exercise, remember that the idea is to keep rotating to get a feel for the full body coil and uncoil. It may feel awkward at first, but try it 5 to 10 times. Then, when you return to hitting normal groundstrokes, try to feel the increased body rotation with your strokes.

2. Another consideration when you try this exercise is to shorten your backswing. This will help you become more efficient because proper body rotation is required with a more efficient and controlled swing.

Variations

1. To get a feel for this exercise, try it against a backboard or with a ball machine rather than in a live-ball rally.

2. If you are a high-level player, try this exercise in a game situation. You will benefit from being forced to recover quickly and react effectively under pressure.

3. You can experiment with this drill with four players rallying competitively from the baseline. This exercise can add a dimension of fun and excitement because the players may tactically try to hit two balls in a row to the same player.

4. Once you get a feel for each variation, alternate between taking the full rotation one time and then hitting the next ball with your regular swing. If you stay relaxed through your normal swing, you should get a feel for the circular or angular momentum that allows the top players in the world to generate power with much less effort than average players use.

Ten in a Row

Description

This is a terrific exercise designed to help you recognize the fastest speed at which you can rally with maximum control and consistency. All you need is a partner and a stopwatch or a watch with a second hand. Start the timer and see how much time it takes you and your partner to hit the ball 10 times down the line from baseline to baseline without making a mistake. Although a simple concept, it is quite outstanding because you will quickly gain a reference point for improvement.

Helpful Tips

1. If you have trouble rallying from baseline to baseline, move this exercise in to the service line. Just remember to play it in both directions crosscourt as described in one of the variations.

2. When playing this game crosscourt, don't get complacent and just stand in one place. Remember to recover and move your feet to make the exercise as close as possible to a game situation.

Variations

1. If you're playing with many players, have pairs of players compete to see which pair can complete 10 hits in a row in the shortest time without making a mistake. In this situation, this drill becomes competitive among the pairs of players while it encourages cooperation between the two players on each team.

2. Do this exercise crosscourt in addition to down the line. In fact, consider playing this drill crosscourt more often than down the line because tennis is a game in which most balls are hit crosscourt.

3. Also do this exercise with four players and with other shots. For example, use volleys and a combination of lobs and overheads.

4. For the most advanced players, try this drill with just 6 balls in a row as the goal (after mastering 10). This will encourage the higher-level players to hit harder and harder, certainly the pattern with today's most competitive players.

5. Play out the point after the goal of a certain number is reached. This effectively combines both cooperation and competition in a single game.

8 Adding Machine

Description

This is a game that also can be played both cooperatively and competitively. To make it cooperative, you and a partner rally baseline to baseline. A ball landing inside the service line counts as 1 point; past the service line but in the court counts as 2 points. Just count aloud and see how fast you and your partner can cumulatively get to 100 points.

Helpful Tips

1. The key to the success in this exercise is to count aloud so that even someone on the next court can hear. Especially in the final competitive group variation below, counting loudly is essential to making the drill exciting.
2. For the most advanced players, do not count the first ball fed in each rally.

Variations

1. As with many of the exercises in this section, this one can easily be adapted to beginning or advanced levels of play. Beginners play minitennis and are awarded 2 points for each ball that lands in the service box.
2. For the most advanced players, stretch a rope parallel to the net halfway between the service line and the baseline. Balls that land between the service line and rope count as 1 point and balls that land between the rope and the baseline count as 2.
3. To create a group competition, have many pairs of players perform the same exercise at the same time.
4. To make this same exercise competitive, have each player count aloud (but say only his own score) and see which player gets to 50 points first.

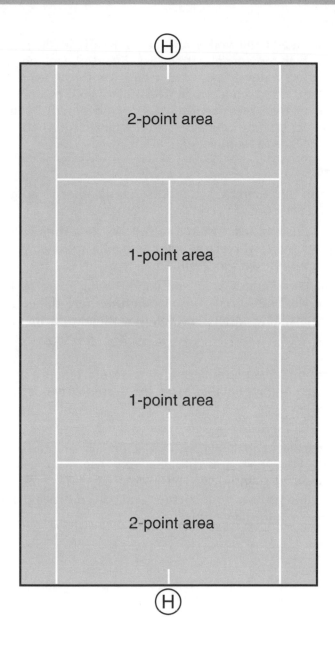

Controlled Scramble

Description

This game is an advanced volley and groundstroke drill. You will need a partner for this high-movement yet cooperative drill. One person stands at the net just hitting volleys. The other stands on the other side of the net alternating volleys and groundstrokes. If you and your partner have perfect control, you can do this exercise without a lot of movement. But in most cases, the volleys will not be fully controlled, so the player alternating volleys and groundstrokes will need to move quite a bit.

Helpful Tips

1. To perform this exercise with control, remember to arc the ball sufficiently over the net.
2. Establish a goal of just five in a row at first and then go for 10. It may sound easy, but it will take some practice for most players to develop enough control to be successful.
3. This drill also doubles as a great conditioning exercise. Realize, however, that the more tired you become the more difficult it will be to control the ball. Be patient and rotate with your partner frequently.

Variations

1. As a warm-up skill builder to this exercise, start on the service line and play this game minitennis style to gain the control needed to succeed on the full court.
2. Perform this exercise crosscourt as well.
3. For an even bigger challenge, you and your partner alternate volleys and groundstrokes. Start with this challenge from the service line with minitennis, and then move back to the baseline. This variation will certainly help you and your partner gain ball control and increase your fitness levels at the same time.

Winner, or Forced Error and Lose

Description

This exercise is guaranteed to establish control and consistency while disarming the multitude of overhitters who populate the recreational ranks. Points start with a serve as in normal tennis. However, in this drill, the player who hits a winner or even forces an error loses the point. In case of doubt, the player who misses the shot makes the decision whether it was a forced or unforced error. The result is a series of very long points, which force players to learn world-class patience. Play competitively with regular scoring.

Helpful Tips

1. As you develop patience along with ball control, you must also be conscious of where your balls are landing. See where your opponent is standing to see whether your shots will be effective in real play. If your opponent is well behind the baseline to return your balls, you can be confident you are becoming an effective tactician and player.

2. On the other hand, if your opponent is consistently moving inside the baseline to return your shots, rest assured you will be in big trouble in a match. If your balls are landing short, try increasing the arc of your shots over the net. Often this simple adjustment will take care of your problems. Visualize a bright yellow horizontal line three feet above the net, and hit each ball over it.

Variations

1. You can also play this exercise cooperatively simply by counting how many balls you and a partner can hit consecutively.

2. Like many of the exercises in this chapter, this drill allows you to isolate specific shots and also specific directions. For example, you can start with forehands only crosscourt, then move to backhands only crosscourt, and then move to random play by using the entire court.

3. For the most advanced players, you can even require all balls to land behind the service line. If a ball lands short, the player who hits it loses that point.

Two Bounces Inside the Baseline

Description

This practice exercise works wonders for beginners who need extra time to prepare for the ball, for seniors who may have trouble running as fast as they used to, and for stronger players who are inconsistent because they have a habit of hitting too hard. It also quickly helps all players develop softer hands and ball control. You and your partner start in the backcourt and cannot cross in front of the baseline. Your goal is to hit softly enough so that the balls bounce twice inside the singles half court, down the line.

Helpful Tips

1. Players will take a smaller backswing as an initial response to this drill. The real answer, however, is to take a normal backswing but swing much more slowly. This will be challenging for most players.

2. Several companies now produce slower-bouncing balls that are perfectly suited for this drill and help you gain more ball control in general. Foam balls are another option.

Variations

1. Start by playing this game cooperatively with a goal of hitting a certain number in a row, such as 10 or 20.

2. You can also play this competitively, scoring one point each time your ball bounces two times inside the baseline on the opposite side of the net. Remember, however, if the ball bounces more than twice, no points are scored. You are also not allowed to step onto or inside the baseline.

3. In addition to playing this game down the line, try it crosscourt in both directions, and then use the full court, allowing for random angled patterns of play.

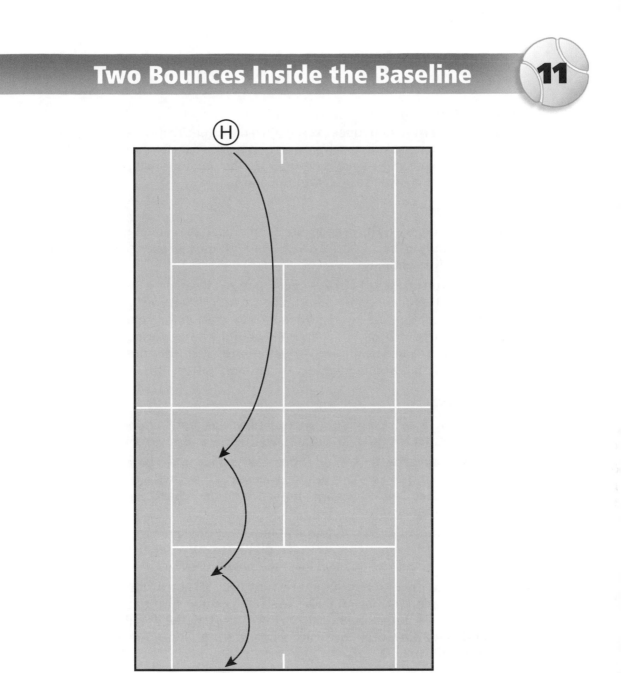

12 Stand Behind the Baseline

Description

This drill takes the two-bounce exercise just described to its next logical level. In this drill you must keep your partner behind the baseline, and the ball can bounce only once in the singles court. As in the previous drill, you and your partner are not allowed to step into the court.

Helpful Tips

1. Even players who have good ball control need to remember to take a full swing during these control drills. Short, choppy strokes typically result in inconsistent play.

2. When you take short strokes every time you want extra control, you will also do this under under pressure in a match. When you tighten up, balls land shorter in the court, which is an invitation for your opponent to take charge of the point. Therefore, take full swings during these control drills and regulate ball speed to gain control by slowing down your swing rather than becoming tighter and more tentative.

Variations

1. As in the last exercise, you can play this both cooperatively and competitively as well as both down the line and crosscourt.

2. As you advance, hit behind ropes that you lay down parallel to the net between the service line and the baseline. This visual aid will guide you to hit deeper and deeper shots, which are characteristic of more advanced play.

3. For players of slightly different abilities, lay down the ropes in different positions to force the stronger player to hit deeper than the less competent player; this will level the playing field.

4. Combine the concept of the previous drill (#11) with this drill. In this case, have one player make the ball bounce two times inside the baseline while the other controls the ball so it bounces only once. Then, add all of the variations just described for hours of fun and effective practice.

Description

This exercise is driven by the use of a 42-foot rope or bungee strung across the net. Just secure broomsticks or telescopic poles to the net posts, and tie the rope from pole to pole to increase the height of the net. Although incredibly simple, this visual aid yields tremendous results in terms of ball control and consistency. It is also a great equalizer if players are of slightly different ability. Play a set in which you require all balls to travel over the raised net, with the exception of the serve, which can go over or under.

Helpful Tips

1. Typically, players trying to arc the ball higher over the net think in terms of swinging their rackets more from low to high. However, hitting over a primary target such as a rope several feet above the net leads to the same result automatically. Don't think about the path of your racket when performing this drill; just think about clearing the line above the net. Then, almost magically, you will have slightly adjusted your swing without even thinking about it.

2. You will observe that your balls land consistently behind the service line, at least much more than normal. As a simple rule of thumb, the higher the ball arcs over the net, the deeper it lands in the court.

Variations

1. The possible variations for this concept are endless. You can create cooperative or competitive drills to isolate specific strokes, directions, and even spin. The main issue of each of them, however, should be to gain a solid understanding of net clearance and control.

2. Play a game of controlled doubles in which the players hit all balls over the doubled net. Make it mandatory that all serves go over the raised net. This will ensure that all players spin their serves.

3. You can also adapt this concept to level the playing field if you and your partner are of significantly unequal abilities. Have the stronger player hit all balls over the higher net and the weaker player can hit anywhere at all.

14 Microtennis

Description

This ball-control drill is simple but simultaneously difficult enough to challenge players at almost every level. Line up with your partner across the net from you and hold onto the net with your nonracket hands. Hit only backspin and you will quickly realize that this is a great skill builder for both drop shots and counter-drop shots.

Helpful Tips

1. Remember that this is a cooperative drill and is not to be performed competitively.
2. If controlling the ball back and forth over the net is too difficult at first, one of you can toss the ball to the other so that only one player is using a racket. Then, gradually try hitting the ball back and forth.

Variations

1. Set goals, such as 10 balls in a row, but make sure that both you and your partner are holding onto the net at all times.
2. One player or both can hit drop volleys, or both players can alternate back and forth between drop shots and drop volleys—of course while still holding the net.
3. Add movement by having one player (or ultimately both) hit the drop shot and run back to touch the service line in between hits. When this variation is competitive, it is one of the most challenging control drills you can find. Both you and your partner will be hustling like crazy to out-drop-shot each another.

Rock-Solid Stroke Mechanics

Tennis practice is divided into three main categories: blocked, serial, and random. Simply put, blocked practice is repetitive practice with emphasis on one particular stroke or aspect of the game. Serial practice is just as it sounds: practicing a combination of shots and repeating that sequence over and over. Random is practicing in an unpredictable, gamelike environment.

Currently in tennis coaching, there is a major emphasis on the benefits of random practice. Although much can be said to extol reality-based, or random, practice situations, at times blocked practice is necessary for developing a specific skill.

Always keep in mind, however, why the blocked practice is taking place and the game situations in which the practiced skill will be ultimately used. In fact, it is not only a good idea to try out the game situation first, but it is also essential. Otherwise, how do we know what skills need more isolated work in the first place? All too often coaches assume that a student needs to work on a specific skill without seeing how well that skill might work in a real-life play situation. This is similar to a car mechanic who assumes that a car needs a tune-up without even turning on the engine to hear how it runs.

Many of the blocked practice games in this chapter can be expanded into dozens of variations, one for each situation in the game. After you isolate a particular skill or situation that you need to work on, use your imagination to create a specific drill designed to meet your personal needs.

Marat Safin is an example of exceptionally rock-solid stroke mechanics—a skill that led him to win the 2000 U.S. Open Championships.

Groundstroke Isolation

Description

This game is an exercise for four players. With all four of you on the baseline, two on each side of the net, one team can hit only forehands and the other team can hit only backhands. This game not only emphasizes one particular stroke but also helps players recognize that backhands are often more controlled and consistent than forehands. If any player or team comes to the net, they must hit only that assigned shot, but this time it becomes either the forehand volley or backhand volley. This rule applies to regular overheads or backhand overheads as well. Points can either start with a serve or with a bounce hit.

Helpful Tips

1. This game effectively pits the attacking nature of the forehand against the controlled style of most backhands.
2. Players will learn to watch their opponents more carefully to take advantage of any situation in which they are out of position.

Variations

1. This game also can be played with two players in a singles format.
2. Have the players in a two-on-one format. In this variation, allow the individual player to hit anything, but the team is allowed to hit only forehands or backhands.
3. For less advanced players, net play may be too challenging. In this event, drop shots are not allowed. If playing competitively, define a drop shot as any ball that would bounce two times inside the service boxes. The team that hits such a short ball, either intentionally or unintentionally, loses the point.
4. Allow one shot on the "wrong" side to be hit per player per point. This variation works well for all levels of play, and it helps players decide when they need this extra bend in the rules to keep them in the game. It also helps the players to be more aware of their opponents' situation and how and when to try to exploit them.

16 Mixed Groundstroke Isolation

Description

This is a doubles variation of the groundstroke isolation drill. Each player on a team is assigned to hit a different groundstroke from her partner. For example, on each team one player can hit only forehands and the partner can hit only backhands. You can consider eliminating drop shots, but to make it challenging, let the teams come to the net, but allow them only forehand or backhand volleys and even regular or backhand overheads, depending on which groundstroke they are allowed. Points can either start with a serve or with a bounce hit.

Helpful Tips

1. The question always arises in doubles about which player should be on the deuce side and which should play the ad. There is no definitive rule, and the consensus of the tennis experts is that players should always figure out what is best for them.

2. One of the benefits of this drill is that players can focus on one shot, isolating either an existing strength to enhance or a weakness to improve. In any case, all players will have to be active to succeed.

Variations

1. This drill works great as well with the two-on-one theme of the previous exercise.

2. For less advanced players, net play may be too challenging. In this event, drop shots are not allowed. If playing competitively, define a drop shot as any ball that bounces two times inside the service boxes. The team that hits such a short ball, either intentionally or unintentionally, loses the point.

3. Allow one shot on the "wrong" side to be hit per player per point. This variation works well for all levels of play and helps players decide when they need this extra bend in the rules to keep them in the game. It also helps the players to be more aware of their opponents' situation and how and when to try to exploit them.

Description

This drill is not only a great exercise for developing confidence in particular shots under pressure, but it also helps players improve reflexes. Players alternate feeding balls from the net to a hitting partner, with the hitter standing in the alley on the baseline, facing away from the net. When the ball bounces, the feeder calls out the hitter's name; the hitter then spins and hits, aiming over the net into the opposite alley. Play this game until the hitter accurately places a predetermined number of shots in the target area.

Helpful Tips

1. For safety, make sure the feeders do not stand directly in the intended flight path of the ball.

2. This drill works well for players of all levels. The only adjustment for those just starting out is to have hitters start closer to the net and the feeders call out their names earlier. If you are a beginner you can also try this exercise in the singles half court, as close to the net as the service line.

Variations

1. For a challenge, try the drill with volleys.

2. Try the exercise with overheads.

Did you know?

In the world of fitness and conditioning there's a technique called *overspeed training.* This means exaggerating resistance or effort to reach a new threshold of speed and power. The spin-and-hit drill is similar in the sense that time, or the shortage of it, is one of the main challenges a player faces on a tennis court. This exercise puts pressure on you to react to an incoming ball in less time, thereby preparing you for the realities of an open sport like tennis. Many of the chapters of this book focus on issues related to this very point: anticipation, decision making, and reflexes.

18 Confident, High, Short Forehands

Description

This basic exercise demonstrates the training concept of *isolation drilling,* another name for blocked practice. In this particular pattern, you and your partner alternate introducing a high, short-bouncing ball to one another that the other player tries to put away. The feed can be hit anywhere, and the hitter must begin behind the baseline.

Helpful Tips

Allow the hitter to reject any fed ball that is too difficult. The objective here is to build confidence.

Variations

1. Turn this into a competitive singles drill. The feeder starts on the baseline to feed a short ball. Then, give the hitter 2 points if the feeder cannot even touch her first shot. All other points count as 1 point for the winner. You can play games until one player reaches 11 points, but give the feeder a head start or handicap by starting him in the lead at 5 points to 0.

2. With minor adjustments you can also turn this concept into an active and exciting doubles drill. Start four players on the baseline and play games to 11, 15, or 21 points. Have each team feed 5 points each and rotate as in table tennis.

Description

This exercise requires three players or, ideally, two players plus a ball machine, because a ball machine can deliver very consistent feeds. One player (or a ball machine) is on one side of the net feeding balls precisely down the middle of the court. The two remaining players start in each of the baseline corners and then alternate hitting groundstrokes to targets across the net in their half of the court. After each shot, the players recover to touch their starting point at the corner of the baseline. Play sets of 30 balls, which allow each player to hit 15. This drill adds conditioning and movement to blocked practice.

Helpful Tips

1. The success of this exercise depends on consistently placed and consistently timed feeds.
2. Ball machines are much better for this drill than human feeds, which are typically difficult to time and place consistently enough for this drill to run smoothly.
3. This is one exercise that doesn't need a technologically advanced ball machine to work perfectly. No spin, no power, and no oscillation—you just need consistent feeds down the middle for a dynamic exercise.

Variations

1. With more than two players, you can rotate either one or two players into this drill every 10 to 15 balls, thus simulating match play in which the longest points rarely last longer than a handful of hits per side per point.
2. For the most advanced players, have both baseline players hit only forehands. This means that one (or both if one is left-handed) will be running around the middle of the court to hit each shot. With this variation, you will have only to make sure to set the feeds slow enough to make it possible for each player to recover to her own corner in between each shot.

20 Ball Machine Poach Volleys

Description

This drill has the same basic setup as the previous drill, with only one difference: The players will now work on their poach volleys. You and your practice partner start on the side T on either side of the court and alternate closing in toward the net to hit the volley. We say "closing in" because after each hit you also have to touch the top of the center strap with your racket. Then, as in the previous exercise, quickly recover to your starting point on the side T. Practice sequences should last 10 feeds (that is, five for each player). A target area should be set up down the middle of the court on the opposite side because this is a simulation exercise for doubles.

Helpful Tips

1. The key to success with this drill is a consistent, well-timed feed.
2. Although the games and drills in this chapter are in the category of blocked practice, you will notice that they are presented in the context of a real play situation. As you practice, think of each exercise in this way to effectively increase your focus and to properly prepare you for the real thing.

Variation

This exercise works best with more than two players. But remember that it is best to rotate players after five hits. Tennis practice sessions in which each player hits only one ball and then goes to the end of the line are not considered satisfactory because if your one shot happens to be an error, you have no opportunity to learn from the mistake and make any adjustments.

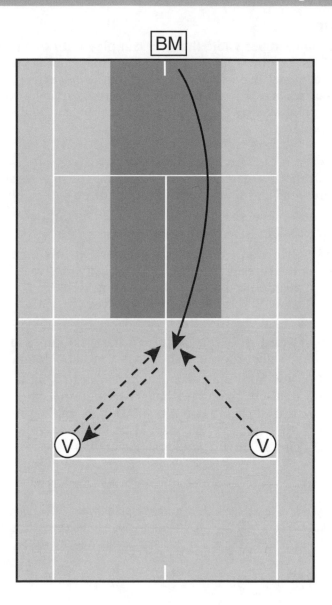

BM

V   V

Use Your Big Weapon

Description

This is a baseline singles game that you can play until one player or team reaches 11, 15, or 21 points. Before starting, each player must pick one weapon (for example, a forehand, backhand, or volley) and advise the opponent of the selection. If you win a point with the weapon of your choice, you are awarded 3 points. Any point won by a shot different from the announced selection is worth just 1 point.

Helpful Tips

1. This is an effective game-based drill because the players start to realize their strengths and try to use them more often.
2. The savviest players will be careful to avoid an opponent's strength as much as possible.
3. You will notice that everyone's movement in this drill will increase because of the rules, which will automatically motivate the players to move into position to hit their chosen shot.

Variations

1. This game-based drill can be turned into a doubles drill, but both players must select the same shot as their weapon of choice.
2. A variation for both singles and doubles is to spin a racket at the beginning of each game and have two optional shots with which everyone can try to score bonus points. For example, spin a racket, and if it is "up" the shot of choice would be forehand groundstrokes and forehand volleys; "down" would be backhands.

Strategy

Far too often, players at all levels cannot answer the simple question, "With what shot do you win most of your points?" Players need to ask themselves this question every time they step onto a court to compete. This task will refocus your attention on which shot you want to hit as often as possible.

Description

Solid contact, which can be felt as well as heard, is the essence of successful tennis play at all levels. You will probably find it easier to make solid contact with one groundstroke over the other. Bring a bath towel to the court and find a trusting player to hold the towel as a matador would hold a cape in a bullfight. The objective is to hit the towel with the racket at the same position that you would hit an actual tennis ball. Start slowly and safely but take a full forehand or backhand swing. The solid contact of the racket with a towel will make a very loud popping sound. Practice this exercise until you can alternate forehand and backhand groundstrokes with a consistently solid feel and sound of contact on both sides.

Helpful Tips

1. Before swinging at full speed, try a few slow-motion strokes to eliminate any chance of hitting the player holding the towel. Of course, make sure the holder stands still while holding the towel to his side.

2. If you're the person holding the towel, make sure the person holding the racket is someone you can trust.

Variations

1. Once you can consistently create a loud popping sound while standing still, try moving around the court. For example, the towel holder might be on or near the singles sideline. Then, you (as the hitter) take a split step in the middle of the baseline and move over to hit the towel.

2. For a more advanced sequence, several towel holders can be in different positions on the court. Try setting up three towel holders—two on the baseline, with one at each of the connections of the singles sidelines, and the third person in the midcourt area—simulating what would happen when the baseliner moves in to knock off a short ball for a winner. Now the hitting player (the person with the racket about to spank the ball) pretends that three balls in sequence are being hit from across the net. The first feed goes to one baseline corner and the second to the other corner; the third is short to the midcourt.

Did you know?

Most balls, even when hit with topspin or backspin, are contacted with the racket face perpendicular to the ground. With topspin, for example, many players make the mistake of trying the impossible—to "turn" the racket face over the ball during the few milliseconds when the ball is actually on the strings. The result is less control and many errors. Instead, to generate topspin, simply keep the racket face perpendicular to the ground. Then, swinging from low to high, create a brushing up motion on the ball by starting the swing from low beneath the contact point and finishing high above it.

Sizzling Serve and Return of Serve

In game-based learning, as discussed in the introduction to this book, even beginning players want to play games right off the bat, even if it means tapping the serve in from the service line to get things started! Surprisingly, even intermediate and advanced players tend to drill far too often without starting each point with a serve. This is quite a paradox because the first shot of every single point in tennis is a serve, and the next shot is inevitably the return. Plus, a large percentage of points never get to a rally situation anyway.

The game-based drills in this chapter center on the serve and return for a very good reason. These are simply the two most important shots in the game because they are the most frequently hit.

Bombs away! Venus Williams looks cool as she prepares to return serve, but she introduced many of the fastest serves and most aggressive returns ever recorded in women's tennis.

Description

This is a match simulation drill that emphasizes attacking weak serves. The rule modification to force this behavior is to give the server only one serve that must be hit underhanded. Immediately you'll see the receiver move inside the baseline and assume a much more confident, aggressive, and offensive posture. A secondary benefit is the server's increased focus because holding a serve will be much more difficult. Play a regular set of singles.

Helpful Tips

1. To stay in the game, the server will be forced to recover quickly to the correct court position, as explained in the next exercise.
2. In some situations, if the receiver is hitting many outright winners, the server will have to begin guessing and moving toward one sideline or the other after hitting the serve.

Variations

1. Play doubles with the same rules.
2. Instead of serving underhanded, serve regular overhand but with the back knee on the ground. Still allow only one serve.
3. Try this drill with one serve from a cross-legged sitting position.
4. Serve from a position lying on your back with your feet pointed toward the net. But, with this one, you'd better get up in a hurry!

Serve and Touch

Description

The server has a more daunting task than is commonly understood. After each serve, you must recover and get in the right position *before* the receiver contacts the ball. Play a set of singles; however, after each serve, the server must touch one of the two singles sidelines with the racket. Servers must stand in their normal serving positions. The purpose is twofold: to intensify the server's footwork and to identify open-court target areas for the receiver.

Helpful Tips

1. The server should not get so anxious to recover from touching the sideline that it interferes with executing the serve properly.
2. You will find that hitting a spin serve will give you more time to touch the sideline, recover, and then prepare for the next shot.

Variations

1. This drill works both for doubles and singles; however, in doubles, adjust the rules for server to touch the doubles sidelines after serving.
2. In this variation the receiver instead of the server must touch the sideline after hitting the return.
3. The final variation is to have both the server and the receiver touch the sideline (singles or doubles depending on what you are playing).

Strategy

You must assume the correct court position after each serve; however, it can be complex because you have a minimum of six choices when serving to the deuce box and six more when serving to the other side. You have two basic recovery positions side to side and three recovery positions relative to the distance from the baseline. The following are general guidelines when serving to the deuce court.

1. Serve is wide and not too strong (expect a strong return).
2. Serve is wide and reasonably strong (expect a fairly strong return but not overpowering).
3. Serve is wide and extremely strong (expect a weak return).
4. Serve is down the middle and not too strong (expect a strong return).
5. Serve is down the middle and reasonably strong (expect a fairly strong return but not overpowering).
6. Serve is down the middle and extremely strong (expect a weak return).

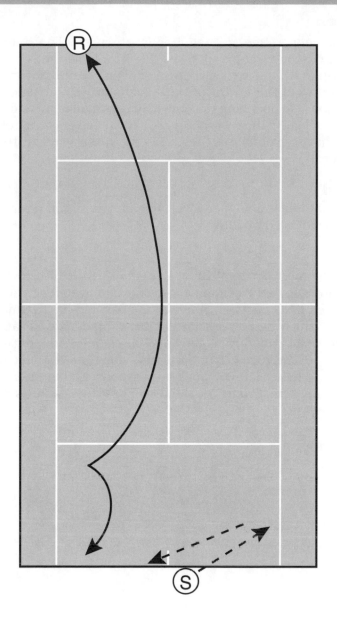

Play It Again, Sam

Description

This game is cooperative and requires four players. The rules focus on a consistent crosscourt return of serve. Play a regular set of doubles with regular scoring with the server allowed only one serve. However, the point does not start until the return of serve lands crosscourt and in. Also, for obvious reasons, no poaching is allowed. Play a regular set of doubles. If the return does not land in the crosscourt area, the receiver gets another chance. However, if the receiver misses three in a row, the server wins that point and play continues.

Helpful Tip

Remember that this is a cooperative game only until the return goes crosscourt, and then it is competitive.

Variation

As you become more accomplished, after the serve is hit allow the server's partner to move up to the center service line and even reach across the line with the racket. If the partner can reach the ball and hit a winner, that team wins the point. But if the server's partner just contacts the ball and gets it into play, then the point is merely played out. This exercise not only increases the concentration of the receiver but will also fine-tune the placement of the returns because there is now a smaller crosscourt target. But remember the returns must be hit crosscourt and the server's partner cannot step across the center service line.

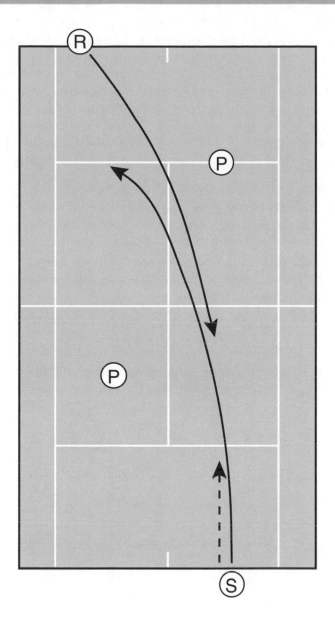

Volleyball Serving

Description

This is a game-based exercise that will help you focus on momentum, a key issue in successful tennis. In this game, you and a practice partner compete but score only the server's points as in volleyball. In other words, if you are serving and win the point, you continue serving. However, if the receiver wins the point, no point is scored; but the receiver regains the serve. As long as the server wins the point, alternate serving to the deuce and ad courts. Play games until one side wins 11 points, and then rotate sides and play again.

Helpful Tips

1. A statistic in competitive tennis shows that the player or team who wins the first 2 points of any game has an 80 percent chance of winning that game. This simple fact shows how important it is not only to gain momentum while playing tennis but also to get it early in each game.

2. After playing this drill, try playing some regular games and attempt to intentionally transfer your sense of the importance of momentum from this drill to regular match play.

Variations

1. This game works as well for doubles as it does for singles.

2. You can also play this game as "receiver volleyball," in which points are scored only when the receiver wins the point.

Description

This singles drill will increase your awareness of gaining early momentum. Play a set with your goal as the receiver to win the first 2 points of a game. When you do, you immediately win the game and become the server. All other games are finished with normal scoring.

Helpful Tips

1. At recreational levels, the player who reaches 30 points first wins 80 percent of the games played. Therefore, this drill focuses on getting the receiving players to win the first 2 points played in each game.

2. A benefit of this drill is that you notice that your focus will increase, and your play will become more aggressive when you are the receiver.

Variations

1. Play the same game, but reward the servers for winning the first 2 points instead of rewarding the receivers for winning the points.

2. Award the games to either the server or the receiver, whichever player can win the first 2 points in a row.

3. This game works just as well for doubles as it does for singles.

Strategy

The percentage of service games won increases as your tennis improves. This means that the importance of breaking serve increases as well. Keep in mind that this is more significant in doubles than in singles. The reason is that service games in doubles are won much more than in singles because the serving team has the first opportunity to take charge of the net and win points. If you need to be convinced of this pattern, just look at the scores in doubles tournaments. Many more sets are determined by tiebreakers in doubles than in singles because all players win a high percentage of their service games. The point is that winning the first points of each game is important and becomes even more critical as your game improves.

180-Degree Return

Description

This exercise is a creative way for you to improve your reflexes for the return of serve while at the same time shortening any oversized backswings. You and a partner play a set of singles. The receiver on the baseline starts facing the back fence. Then, as soon as the receiver hears the noise of the serve being hit, it's time to turn and hit the return.

Helpful Tips

1. Consider giving the server just one serve because the receiver may need a little extra time initially to make the turn before returning the serve.
2. The receiver must be very alert to succeed in this drill. This skill will help any player return serves better under any conditions.

Variations

1. This game also works well for doubles.
2. With four players on the court, you can have both players on the receiving team face away from the server for an extra challenge.
3. Have the server's partner at the net also turn around, only to spin and face the net upon hearing the receiver contacting the ball.

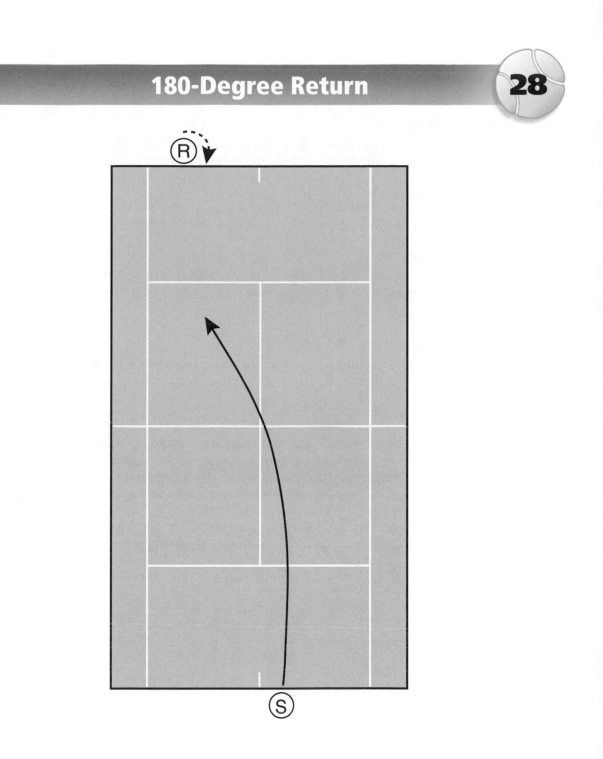

360-Degree Return

Description

This exercise is an extension of the previous drill to help you improve your reflexes for returning the serve. It is also helpful if you need to shorten your backswing. You and your practice partner alternate serving to each other. The receiving player on the baseline now makes a 360-degree turn as soon as the server tosses the ball to serve. Then, after completing the spin, the receiver hits the return. Sound simple? Play a set this way and find out for yourself.

Helpful Tip

The only rule adjustment you may want to consider is to give the server just one serve because the receiver may need a little extra time to make the turn.

Variations

1. This game also works well for doubles.
2. To increase the intensity of the drill, add a rule that the receiver must stand inside the baseline to perform the turn and return the serve.

Did you know?

Andre Agassi is recognized as one of the best receivers in the world, if not the best in the entire history of tennis. He sees the ball early, prepares with a compact swing, explodes forward into the ball, and returns with uncanny accuracy (as well as power) against the world's best servers. Isn't it strange that recreational players actually make the return of serve much more complicated than a player as talented as Agassi? At recreational levels, the servers hit the ball more slowly, and they tend to serve in consistent and predictable patterns. Yet a huge percentage of recreational players (more men than women) take a bigger backswing than Agassi does. If you can execute this drill and the previous exercise (#28) consistently after just a little practice, it probably means that your backswing is not too big. However, if you continue to spray the ball all over the place, understand that your backswing is probably too large.

Jump-Start the Receiver

Description

Many competitive tennis players find it difficult to concentrate consistently during a match. In this exercise, you and a partner play a set while starting all games at 30-0 for the receiver. The purpose is to put pressure on the server to compete at a more focused level to hold serve. This game should also help the receiver maintain concentration because a 30-0 lead makes it clear that the receiver should win those games.

Helpful Tip

Make sure the server calls out the score loudly and clearly at the beginning of each game. This will help increase the focus of both players.

Variations

1. Start all games at 30-0 in favor of the server, putting pressure on the receiver to rise to a higher level in attempting to break serve.
2. Doubles is a good option for the first variation.
3. This, like many of the drills and games in this book, can be used for social tournaments as well as for practice sessions.

Strategy

Tennis has two basic objectives: Hit the ball over the net and hit it inside some lines. When you hit the ball over the net, realize that you have accomplished 50 percent of your goals! This simple point will help anyone play better tennis in seconds. It is especially true about serving and returning serve. From a serving perspective, one of the worst things you can do is to hit your first serve in the net and then hit your second serve in the net as well. You didn't even give gravity a chance! From a receiving perspective, don't think you always have to hit great returns to win tennis matches. Just get the ball back consistently, and you always have a chance that your opponent will make an error.

Serve With a Snap

Description

This exercise helps improve the racket acceleration on your serve. Although this book is geared almost exclusively toward game-based drills rather than individual shots, this exercise is important because the serve does, after all, begin every single point in tennis. Stand on the baseline and snap down so hard that the ball bounces on your own side of the court first before clearing the net. As you advance, work on more and more wrist acceleration to eventually snap down with tremendous velocity so that each ball bounces on your side of the court and then immediately hits the opposing back fence. If you can't reach the back fence, then challenge yourself to get the second bounce to land as close to the end of the court as possible.

Helpful Tip

To execute this drill properly, make sure to relax your grip on the racket as much as possible. You may even want to drop one or two fingers off the bottom of the racket handle.

Variations

1. With more than one player, create a competition by seeing how many consecutive serves can hit the back fence within a two- or three-minute period. If the back fence is not a realistic goal, set an achievable target such as reaching the opposing baseline.

2. Another variation is snapping your wrist in the opposite direction—up. To try this exercise, stand on the baseline and serve so that your ball hits the opposite back fence (better yet, try to hit over it) on a fly.

True Story

Tennis celebrity John McEnroe was on the *Late Show With David Letterman* before the 2001 U.S. Open. McEnroe was filmed standing on a rooftop in New York City, where it happened to be raining at the time. Across the street a few floors down from him was an open window into which he was supposed to serve a tennis ball. He had three chances. The first missed high and to the right by about three feet. The second missed low and to the left by maybe a foot. And, you guessed it, on his third attempt, he cracked another serve and the ball flew cleanly through the middle of the open window. McEnroe looked quite relieved because he knew he was on national television. But, for me, what was interesting to see were the adjustments he made with his wrist to get the ball into its target. The first was high and to the right, so McEnroe adjusted the second low and to the left, and the third threaded the needle. Well done, John McEnroe!

Just Forehand Returns

Description

This game-situation drill emphasizes forehand return of serve. In this game, you and your practice partner play a set of singles with two rules governing play: The server has only one serve per point, and the receiver is allowed to hit only forehand returns. The rules of this game will automatically help you develop your service return into more of a weapon.

Helpful Tip

To effectively run around your backhand on the return of serve, keep your feet moving as much as possible. This drill also helps you develop your movement skills, balance, and agility.

Variation

This drill can be used for doubles as well as singles and obviously fits directly into the trends of today's tennis.

33 Two Returns Per Point

Description

This exercise focuses on developing confidence on the return of serve. Play a set of singles with your partner, but the server gets only one serve and the receiver gets two chances at getting the serve back in play. In other words, the receiver is allowed to miss the first return and still get another chance; the server has to serve another ball to the same box. This training drill takes the pressure off the receiver and puts it on the server. It forces consistent serves and encourages the receiver to go for bigger and bigger shots. And, because the server will be hitting mostly second serves, the receiver will get a mind-set of attacking all second serves because they are usually a little slower and easier to handle.

Helpful Tip

Receivers should stick with consistent patterns of returning. They should not be aggressive for the first return and ease up on the second one. Rather, try to commit to a return and stick with the plan.

Variation

This drill works for doubles as well as for singles.

Three-Point Shots

Description

This exercise can add a lot of fun to any practice session. The only requirement is to bring one different-colored ball to the court in addition to the standard yellow balls. As you will see, the rules create a wild-card environment that makes every game more interesting. On any first or second serve during a game, the server can pull that different-colored ball out of his pocket, and that particular point is immediately worth 3 points. In other words, if the server won the first point of the game and the score is 15-0, winning the next point with the colored ball would end the game. However, if the receiver wins that point, the score would be 15-40. With this rule in place you'll be amazed to see how much the receiver's focus increases in anticipating the return and how much both players increase their concentration in general.

Helpful Tip

If you don't have a ball of a different color, you can also use a magic marker to color a ball. Just let the ink dry before putting it in your pocket!

Variations

1. For better players with booming first serves, allow the differently colored ball to be used only on second serves.
2. To tilt the balance in favor of the receiver, make it mandatory for the server to use that ball once per game on any serve; but make it only a 3-point possibility for the receiver.
3. This idea works well for doubles in addition to singles.
4. You can add the rule that the receiver must chip and charge when a colored ball is served.
5. The server must serve and volley when using the colored ball.
6. Any of these ideas work well for social tournament events. Rule adjustments like these are guaranteed to spice things up for everyone involved.

35 Two-Ball Serving

Description

For years this has been one of my favorite doubles drills. The rule modification is to have both members of the serving team serve at the same time. In other words, they each have one ball and stand on the baseline to serve to opposite service boxes. After that, anything goes. However, they get only one serve each; therefore, if they both miss their serves it is counted as a double fault. Also, the receivers must not return out balls because if one of the serves lands in the box, play begins, and it can be distracting. If one of the serves lands in the net and the other one goes in the correct box, the ball that lands in is the ball that is played out by all four players. Points are determined by which team wins the last ball in play. For several hits, two balls may be in play at the same time. This drill is fun, fast, and exciting; it will also increase focus and build reflexes.

Helpful Tips

1. For safety, the servers are not allowed to serve and volley unless the receivers are required to hit the first balls back crosscourt.

2. Both servers must hit their serves at approximately the same time.

3. The servers will switch positions so that they are each serving to different boxes after each point.

Variation

This is one exercise that needs no variations to keep interest high. You can have fun playing this drill nearly every day for the rest of your career.

Creative Spin and Specialty Shots

Blow up a beach ball and hold it in front of you with both hands, lining up the colored segments side to side. Then experiment with creating the two basic spins in tennis: *topspin* (also known as forward spin) and *backspin* (also known as underspin). Topspin can be likened to the wheels of a car traveling forward. Backspin is the opposite. After you get the feel for creating these two different ball rotations, spin the ball both ways without a bounce to a partner or against a wall about 10 feet away. Notice the difference in the trajectory created by each spin. With topspin, the beach ball will travel forward in the air and then dip dramatically before bouncing. Backspin, on the other hand, will maintain a level path or rise slightly over the course of its flight.

The laws of aerodynamics govern the trajectory of the spin. Let us first consider topspin. When the ball spins forward, it pushes the air forward with it and creates a lower pressure area directly underneath the ball. The ball drops as it travels through the air because of lower air pressure underneath the flying ball. With backspin, the opposite occurs because backspin can slightly reduce the air pressure above the ball, helping it to travel on a level plane longer or even go up slightly, depending on the RPM (revolutions per minute) the ball is traveling.

Every ball in tennis has some degree of spin, whether we intentionally create it or not. And every single ball that bounces on a tennis court comes off the court with topspin. Exactly how much topspin is determined by the type and degree of incoming spin before the bounce.

South Africa's top player Wayne Ferreira is not the most powerful player on the men's tour, but he has proven himself to be very versatile.

We also need to mention the third basic type of spin that is used primarily on the serve: the slice. Slice, or sidespin, is a sideways spin of the ball. A slice serve will move sideways through the air and, with enough sidespin, will even continue its exaggerated flight path after the bounce.

The following are some examples of uses for different types of spin:

- Your opponent is rushing the net or is already there. You want to keep the ball low. Topspin will clear the net and dip to your opponent's feet, forcing your opponent to hit up.

- Your opponent has trouble hitting high backhands from the baseline. Hit topspin groundstrokes with high net clearance to the backhand side and look for a weak or short return.

- Your opponent hits forehand groundstrokes with a continental grip (and probably with a straight arm). This is a sign that your opponent has difficulty hitting forehands at shoulder height or higher (those balls will tend to go long and float high over the net). Your tactic will be to hit high, looping topspin groundstrokes to the forehand side.

- Your opponent is very tall, likes to play from the baseline, and has trouble with low balls. Hit backspin groundstrokes low over the net so that they land around the service line, and watch him struggle to dig your shots out of the dirt.

- Your opponent hits forehand groundstrokes with a full western grip. This is a telltale sign that she has trouble hitting low forehands because the racket face will be very closed (these balls will tend to travel low over the net and land short, if they clear the net at all). Your tactic is to hit backspin groundstrokes low over the net so that they land around the service line.

- Your right-handed opponent hits a two-handed backhand return of serve. In the deuce court, hit your slice down the middle, making it "break" into his body, jamming him on the backhand side. If this doesn't give you a few free points, nothing will.

Along with various spins, you need to be able to hit *specialty shots,* which are ideally executed with one spin or another. Traditionally, we think of drop shots, lobs, and overheads as specialty shots. But counter-drop shots, passing shots, and subspecialties like defensive and offensive lobs are also part of the specialty shots.

The games and drills in this chapter are designed to help you hit various types of spin plus the basic and not-so-basic specialty shots. In many ways, these types of shots are the truly creative part of the sport.

36 Second Bounce (Leave It!)

Description

This is a perspective-changing drill in which you and your practice partner are guided to hit the ball with more depth and more angles (and more topspin for more advanced players). The goal is to make the ball land in the court and then hit either the back or side fence before it bounces twice on the court surface. When you think you have successfully hit the ball so that this will occur, clearly call out loud, "Leave it!" Your practice partner across the net must then let the ball go. If it hits the back or side fence, the player who hit the shot wins the point immediately. On the other hand, if the ball bounces twice without hitting either fence, whoever hit the ball loses the point immediately.

Helpful Tips

1. This drill is a great way to increase your awareness of how much pressure you are actually placing on your opponent.

2. The key to succeeding at this drill is to hit the ball with increasing arc over the net until success is achieved. This will effectively make the ball bounce higher and farther, increasing your chance of hitting the fence before the ball bounces again on the court.

3. As mentioned earlier, more advanced players will also add topspin to increase the distance between the first and second bounces, thereby helping the ball reach one of the fences before it bounces two times.

Variations

1. Play this game in the half court only either down the line or crosscourt to increase focus on each direction, one at a time.

2. Add the rule that if you call out, "Leave it!" before the ball you hit crosses the net, you are gambling to win or lose 2 points instead of just 1.

True Story

I remember playing in the finals of the White Plains, New York, 10-and-under tennis championship at eight years old. My opponent and I ended up in a three-set battle of wills. The match took place before the creation of tiebreakers and lasted more than four hours. Both of us were fighters and had peers and parents watching. We also got sick from the heat. I can also admit that we were both "pushers," meaning we hit high deep balls, one after another, relentlessly. The result was that many points lasted 30 or 40 hits. It was a marathon. The score was something like 6-8, 26-24, and 11-9. Somehow I ended up winning, but it wasn't pretty.

In those days, being called a "pusher" was anything but a compliment. It meant that a player was too afraid to hit the ball hard. Of course, in that age group, it was a winning tactic. However, it is important to note that hitting steady from the baseline with high looping shots has also become a mainstay strategy among European claycourters. Think of the playing style of gritty counterpunching competitors such as the former French Open champion Aranxia Sanchez-Vicario. She could play this drill we call "second bounce" and hang in there with anyone in the world.

Description

This next exercise is for competitive players with particular focus on developing the skills to hit all the possible groundstrokes (high, low, angled, hard, looping, and so on) with both topspin and backspin. You and your partner start points on the baseline with a bounce hit. Designate one of you to hit only topspin and the other to hit only backspin. With focus on only one spin or the other, you'll quickly learn through firsthand experience what possible speeds, angles, arcs, and placements are possible with each ball. Play games until one player reaches 11 or 15 points, and then switch spins. Drop shots are not allowed, and all balls must bounce once on each side of the net.

Helpful Tips

1. Don't be surprised to learn that at very competitive levels the backspin player can break even with or even defeat the topspin player.

2. The player hitting with topspin will have to move much more than the player hitting backspin. Specifically, the backspin player should recognize that moving the topspin player deep and then hitting low and short will make the topspinner work particularly hard.

3. To keep players hitting groundstrokes, the rules do not allow drop shots. To be clear about whether a shot is a drop shot or not, define a drop shot as any ball that bounces twice inside the service line. If it does, it constitutes an automatic loss of point for the player who hit it.

Variations

1. At first, you may want to isolate each specific groundstroke. To accomplish this, just play crosscourt and allow only forehands or backhands to be hit (depending on whether the players are right- or left-handed).

2. This is much more difficult than it sounds: Play only within the service boxes. In this variation, don't worry about drop shots, but still enforce the one-bounce rule.

Three Spin Serves Per Point

Description

This game focuses on the most important shot in tennis: the serve. This drill favors the server by allowing three serves with one stipulation: The server must hit all three serves with spin. In other words, simply pushing the ball into play is not allowed. If anyone tries to slip a "floater" in, the other player has the responsibility to call out, "Floater—I'll take that point, thank you." The purpose is to take the pressure off the server who may either be developing a spin serve or may be trying to hit second serves with more spin, pace, and depth. Of course, if you miss three serves in a row it is now called a triple fault, and you lose the point. Play a regular set of singles.

Helpful Tips

1. To effectively hit spin serves, remember that a loose grip on the racket is essential for allowing the racket to generate the speed necessary to put spin on the ball.

2. One of the best tips you can remember for keeping a loose wrist is to drop your little finger off the bottom of the grip. The squeezing of the fingers on the grip is what tightens the wrist and prevents fast racket head speed.

Variations

1. This game adapts perfectly for doubles because spin serves give the server more time to get to the net, a key to success in doubles.

2. If necessary, allow the players up to four spin serves per point. The idea is to encourage the players to hang in there and keep hitting that spin serve!

Did you know?

It may seem counterintuitive, but hitting an effective spin serve requires the server to swing the racket as fast as, or even faster than, he would on a hard, flat serve. The reason is that effective spin serves require a tremendous amount of revolutions per minute to be effective. A player like Pete Sampras would generate 5,500 RPM on his second serve! Keep in mind that at his peak, Pete would regularly hit second serves at 110 to 115 miles per hour (very fast for second serves). This means that the second serve ball would rotate 50 to 60 times before bouncing in the opposing service box. The combination of speed and spin on his second serve gives him the distinction of having perhaps the most effective second serve in the history of tennis.

Backboard to Practice Overheads

Description

One of the most frequently hit specialty shots is the overhead. However, it is also the least frequently practiced shot. Usually, players hit just the basic strokes—forehands and backhands—against a backboard. But practicing overheads against a backboard is also effective. Start with an abbreviated service motion and snap down enough so that the ball bounces on the ground before it hits the backboard. This makes the ball bounce off the wall the same as a lob from an opponent, inviting you to hit another overhead. If you can control your overheads to bounce first and then hit the wall, you can hit one overhead after another. Try this exercise until you can hit 10 in a row.

Helpful Tips

1. With a relaxed wrist you should be able to snap down to make this exercise work.
2. If you find this exercise difficult, one of the most common problems is gripping the racket too tightly. If this is the case, drop your little finger off the end of the racket to force you to loosen your grip automatically.

Variation

If you have a partner but want to practice this drill anyway, take turns. Then total the number of successful overheads (ones that bounce before hitting the wall) and play until one player reaches 15 or 21 points.

Description

Although this drill is primarily for beginning players who need to develop their volley skills, it is also an appropriate drill for advanced players. Work with a partner and alternate tossing balls to each other's forehand volley. The player tossing the balls calls out "catch" or "hit" immediately after releasing each ball. To perform a catch, let the ball bounce off your racket (with a little underspin), and then catch it with your nonracket hand. A hit is a normal volley hit back to the feeder. As the volleyer becomes more adept at the skill required to perform this exercise, the feeder can delay calling out "catch" or "hit" until the ball is closer and closer to the volleyer. Rotate positions every 10 to 15 feeds.

Helpful Tips

1. The "catch" skill in this exercise is designed to develop your drop volley. This is why even advanced players will benefit from this exercise.

2. You'll quickly notice that the only way to accomplish the "catch" or "hit" skill is to prepare your racket face open in the range of 45 degrees toward the sky.

3. If you are having trouble with this drill, prepare your racket face before the feeder even releases the ball. And remember, the best players will have practically no backswing at all in this exercise.

Variations

1. Try the exercise with backhand volleys.

2. Try the exercise with the feeder bounce-hitting balls from the baseline.

3. With three players forming a team, have one player toss a ball to the volleyer from 10 feet away. If the instruction is to hit or volley the ball, the team scores a point when the feeder catches the volley out of the air. If "catch" is called out, the third player (who is now standing behind the volleyer) tries to catch the ball after the volleyer's racket lightly touches it to score points for the team. Several groups of three players can then compete to see how many points they can score in a designated time, such as 60 seconds.

Bump and Hit

Description

Although this drill is perfect for beginners, intermediate and even advanced players will benefit as well because they will develop the "soft hands" that are indispensable for drop shots and volleys. Start with two teams of two, getting ready to play minitennis doubles in the service boxes. However, before hitting the ball over the net, the team members have to work together and pass the ball to one another. For example, whoever contacts the ball first bumps or taps it up so that it bounces inside the service box. Then their partner moves into position to hit the ball over the net. Think of it as a volleyball game in which one pass is required on each side of the net; the primary difference in this drill is that the ball must bounce. Obviously for this exercise to succeed, all balls must arc and be hit with backspin. Power, of course, is also not allowed. Players learn teamwork, movement, and ball control with backspin. Another benefit of this drill is that all four players on the court will hit the ball during every single point. Nobody will have the chance to stand around. Start with a bounce hit and play until one team reaches 11 points.

Helpful Tips

1. All four players should remember to keep their feet moving because being positioned and balanced definitely helps a player hit the ball with control.

2. If any player hits with too much power, the team on the other side of the net can call a replay with no penalty to either side. Remember that this drill develops the skills of control and direction.

Variations

1. This game can be played cooperatively whereby all players attempt to reach a common goal, such as 10 or 20 balls in a row.

2. This exercise can be played with only two players. In this situation, each player would bump the ball, let it bounce, and then hit it with control over the net.

3. Try this game in a confined area such as crosscourt with either two or four players.

4. More advanced players can also try all of the previous variations with one change: After the first bump up in the air, the ball is not allowed to bounce but must be volleyed with control over the net.

Description

This is a game-based drill designed to develop the drop volley for the player at the net while helping the player at the baseline with anticipation and movement. Pair up with a practice partner; one player stands at the net and one stands on the baseline playing in the singles half court. The baseliner feeds a ball to the net player. Before making contact, the net player may reject the feed if it is too difficult. The volleyer then hits either a drop volley or a penetrating volley, and the point is played until one player reaches 11 points; then players switch roles.

Helpful Tips

1. To develop skill, the volleyer must stand about halfway from the net to the service line at the start of each point. Standing too close is unrealistic because opponents will lob, and standing too far away makes drop volleys too difficult to attempt.

2. Refer to drill 40 in this chapter for an alternative skill builder that will help with the skills needed for this exercise.

Variations

1. As a preliminary exercise, the volleyer hits only drop volleys. In this scenario the baseliner feeds the ball from close to the back fence, then touches that fence before running forward to play out the point.

2. The primary exercise as well as the first variation can be played crosscourt only, isolating each direction, as well as in the full singles court.

3. Turn the primary exercise as well as variation 1 into a doubles drill.

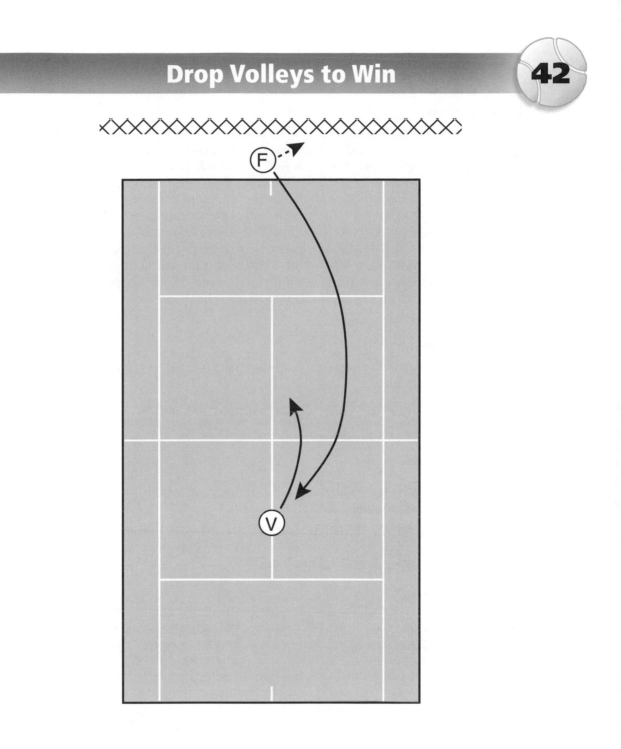

43 Be Creative

Description

Here's an interesting play-situation drill that you can try the next time you are on the court with two friends. This exercise addresses the problem of getting in the rut of hitting the same shots over and over again, resulting in a game so predictable it becomes ineffective. In this drill you are forced to get accustomed to hitting more creative shots: drop shots, topspin lobs, drop volleys, or sharply angled groundstrokes. You and a partner play a tiebreaker. At random, the third player calls out one of the other players' names, who must hit a creative shot, as listed earlier. It is up to that third player to judge whether the shot was a creative attempt or not. If the shot is judged not to be creative, the third player (now in effect the umpire) calls out, "Loss of point," for the player who failed to hit creatively. Rotate among the three players after every tiebreak.

Helpful Tips

1. Limit the instruction for a creative shot to no more than once every three hits for each player.
2. The temporary umpire in this game needs to call out the player's name before the incoming ball crosses the net onto that player's side of the court, not after it bounces.

Variations

1. With only two players, just have one of the players call out "now" for the player across the net.
2. Try doubles if you have five players. Just be aware that in doubles, the umpire will need to focus because the faster play in doubles can make this drill challenging at higher levels.

Did you know?

Chris Evert is one of the greatest players in the history of tennis. She wasn't just great for one or two seasons; her dozens of championship titles spanned more than a decade. Evert's tenacity and stoic focus earned her the nickname "Ice Maiden" early in her career. She was like a backboard—not just consistent—on her groundstrokes. However, after some years on the tour, other players became so familiar with her style that they challenged her more and more. Dennis Ralston was her coach during this period, and he added a well-disguised drop shot to her repertoire. This creative addition quickly became a powerful tactical component in her game until the day she retired from full-time competition.

Reject That Lob

44

Description

This hitting drill focuses on the overhead and lob with a distinguishing starting feature. To prevent this drill from breaking down because the initial lob is too difficult, the net player has the option to reject the feed. Also, the initial overhead must be hit out of the air. Then, after the first overhead, the point is played out. Because high-level players' overheads will be quite strong, you can award 2 points to the baseliner and only 1 point to the net player for points won. Play until one player reaches 11 points, and then rotate positions.

Helpful Tips

1. The player hitting overheads must say, "reject" before the ball bounces on her side of the court. Otherwise, that player would lose the point.

2. The player at the net must start halfway between the net and the service line to keep the drill realistic.

Variations

1. To develop angles on overheads, play this game crosscourt in both directions.

2. You can also convert this game easily into an exciting, high-energy doubles drill.

Strategy

A good nickname for the overhead smash in tennis is the "moment of truth" because losing confidence after missing an overhead can be devastating. The ball is floating high in the air, giving you all the time in the world to set up to smash it away for a winner on a key point. Although it looks easy enough, the loftiest lobs can be among the hardest to hit because the incoming angle often means the ball is coming straight down. It's similar to slow-pitch softball where the pitch is thrown with a high arc and the batter must time a forward swing to connect with a ball that is dropping vertically across the plate. Many batters would prefer a 60-mile-per-hour fastball anytime. So our suggestion is simple: On very high lobs, consider letting the ball bounce. In this game situation, discretion is very much the better part of valor.

Mastering Tactical Skills

Compare using strategy to driving a car on a long trip. If you don't know how to get to your destination, you are certain to get lost. You use tactics to ensure a successful trip: You make sure the car is in good running order (check the fuel level, tire pressure, and oil), know when to make rest stops, stop to eat periodically, and know where you will sleep at night. The overall strategy is having a detailed map and planning how long it will take to make the journey. If you don't plan for these details and more, your "strategy" may turn to tragedy. Can you imagine driving on a highway in the middle of nowhere and getting a flat tire? You think to yourself, *That's OK. I have a spare in the trunk.* So, you change the tire and then lower the car back on the ground only to realize that your spare had no air. Disaster.

In tennis you may have an experience similar to failing to plan for a long trip. You prepare diligently, but you don't bring a second racket; then your string breaks. Or, you are right-handed and prepare your normal game plan of hitting your groundstrokes into your opponent's backhand side, assuming you will be playing a right-hander. It may sound ridiculous, but I have seen players compete and then realize *after* losing that their opponent was left-handed! We need to have an overall strategy to reach our goals. But we also need a back-up plan just in case one of our tires goes flat. You certainly don't want to get stuck without a spare.

The games and drills in this chapter are based on the development of various tactics and strategies. You will use the principle of automatic learning to help you learn the principles of competitive tennis. Automatic learning simply means that, through playing the game or drill, you will learn and improve automatically. The rules of the game guide the behavior that improves performance.

When Martina Hingis hit the pro circuit as a teenager, her superb tactical instincts propelled her to the number one world ranking in no time.

Description

In this exercise, you and your partner start by hitting groundstrokes cross-court. The only time you are allowed to hit down the line is when one of you intends to hit a winner. A down-the-line winner is awarded 2 points. However, if the ball is simply returned, 2 points are deducted from your score. This simple drill emphasizes crosscourt groundstroke patterns and helps players automatically recognize when they can change the ball's direction. Start points with a bounce hit and play games until one player reaches 11, 15, or 21 points.

Helpful Tips

1. All crosscourt groundstroke drills carry the danger of becoming unrealistic: Players often don't bother to recover properly because they know that the ball will be returned crosscourt right back to them. So, focus on recovery and, if necessary, put a spot on the court to touch with your racket in between hits.

2. This game also encourages the player who is returning the down-the-line attempt at a winner just to get the ball back in play. All too often players go for too much when they are under pressure instead of simply neutralizing the point (that is, trying to get the ball back into play).

Variations

1. If you are a beginning player, this variation will allow you to score points more simply. Call out loud "down the line" before hitting the ball in that direction. Then, just for succeeding in hitting it down the line, you score 2 points instead of 1.

2. With advanced players, score 3 points when an absolutely clean winner is hit—one that cannot even be touched by the opponent. Don't try this rule if you are not that experienced because overhitting to score points is not recommended.

3. Have the player returning the attempted down-the-line winner try to hit the ball crosscourt and deep to effectively get back in the point. If that player is successful, award him a 2-point bonus (overall a 4-point gain). This will also put pressure on the player going for the winner to go only for that shot when the percentages are high.

Black Hole

Description

This is a terrific game to help you see the court tactically. You will need four players and two chairs. Place one chair on each center service line, halfway between the service line and the net. One player from each team sits in each chair while the partner plays from the baseline. To win the point, the player in the chair has to volley any ball back into the court. In that event, that seated player rotates positions with her partner on the baseline. This will motivate the seated player to be active in trying to intercept incoming balls. And, more important, it should motivate the baseliner to keep the ball away from the volleyer. After the point is won, the players rotate positions. I suggest starting this game with a bounce hit from the baseline with the team that won the previous point starting the next one.

Helpful Tips

1. Make sure that the types of chairs you use will not scratch the court surface.

2. Make sure that the seated players don't move the chairs around the court.

3. The players sitting in the chairs must keep their pants or skirts in contact with the seat of the chair at all times.

4. Allow the receiving team of the first feed to reject the feed. This keeps overly enthusiastic players from trying to hit outright winners on the first shot.

Variations

1. Less advanced players may be given simpler goals—all the seated player has to do to win the point is to touch the ball with his racket.

2. For more advanced players, adjust the rules so that a point is won simply when any of the players, including those seated, either hits a winner or makes an error. Then, if it happens to be the seated player who won the point for her team, that pair rotates positions.

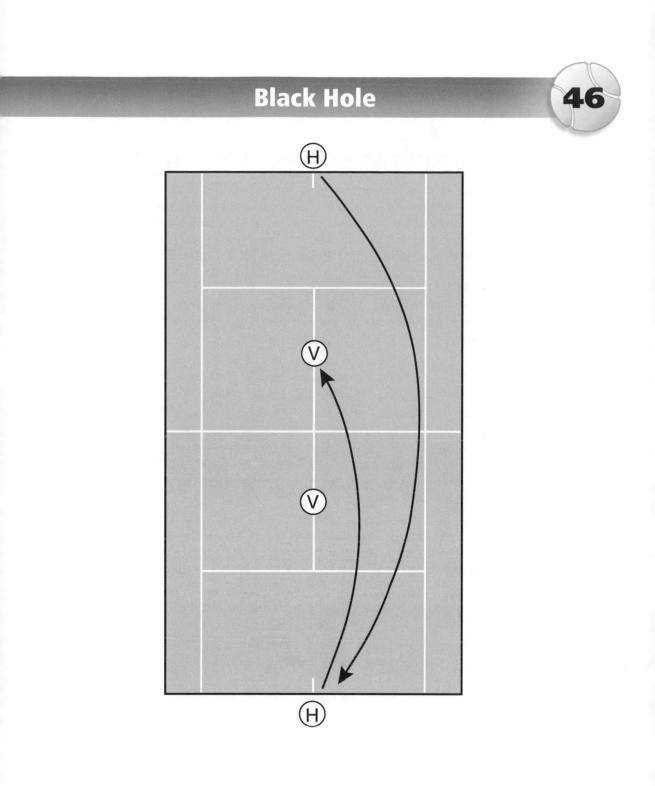

Out of the Middle

Description

This is a variation of the previous drill but with only two players. In this variation, use ropes or throw down rubber curves to create a 15-foot-diameter circle as the area the baseliner must avoid. Any ball that lands in that middle zone loses the point immediately. Start with a bounce hit from the baseline and play out points until one player reaches 11, 15, or 21 points. Whichever player wins each point feeds the next ball. The receiving player can reject the feed in case an overly enthusiastic competitor tries to hit a winner on the first shot.

Helpful Tips

1. The main match strategy for players to learn from this drill is to generally see the balls that land in the middle of the court on their side as opportunities to take charge of the point.

2. The middle area can also be used to handicap the field when a weaker player is pitted against a stronger one. In that case, give the more experienced player a larger middle area to avoid.

Variations

1. This variation is for beginners through intermediate-level players. After the feed, regular points are played out; however, any time the ball bounces in the middle area, play stops immediately with the player who hit the shot losing that point.

2. For more advanced players, each point counts as 1 point. However, each time the ball lands in the middle area, play continues; but the player who hit there loses an additional point. In other words, the scoring is ongoing, and both sides can score or lose points in the middle of each point.

3. Sets of singles can also be played with regular serving and scoring.

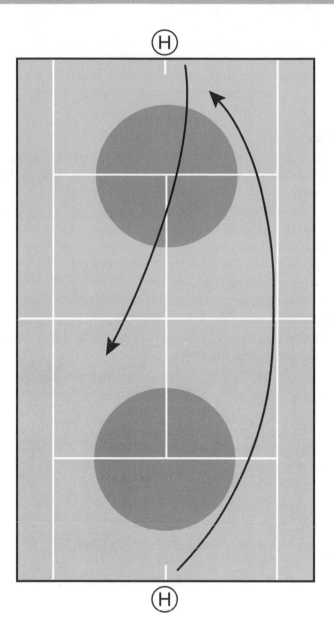

The X Files

Description

This game gets its name from the famous television program "The X Files" because of the crosscourt patterns of play. Start off by hitting forehands crosscourt with a partner and, as soon as the first ball lands short of the service line, you can both immediately use the whole court. Play games until one player reaches 11 points.

Helpful Tips

1. This exercise encourages the player who receives the first short ball to attack (that is, to think about changing the direction of the crosscourt pattern or possibly wrong-footing the opponent).

2. This concept of attacking at the first opportunity is commonly known as "first strike tennis" and is one of the benchmarks of successful play on the professional tour.

Variations

1. To develop confidence on both sides of the court, play the same game with only crosscourt backhands allowed.

2. For more advanced players, add a rule that both players must attack the net immediately after the first short ball.

Strategy

Players understand the principle of attacking short balls in tennis. However, even at the top levels of world-class competition, players seldom take it consistently to the next level—that is, they don't anticipate the short ball based on how deeply they hit their own shots. The ideal strategy is to move inside the baseline as soon as you get your opponent to move farther back from the baseline or to hit any shot outside of his comfort zone.

Double Jeopardy

Description

Here's a game in which you and your partner compete with an emphasis on certain shots. For example, play out singles points, but penalize a mistake on a specific shot more severely than any other mistake. One scenario is that a missed approach shot loses 2 points or, with regular scoring, would mean the loss of the entire game. Although some may find that this drill dwells too much on the negative aspect of missing, it does force players to confront their fears in a competitive situation, which is a must in the quest to develop match toughness.

Helpful Tips

1. There is always the risk of making practice sessions too complicated. Focus on one issue and stick with it for 30 or 60 minutes. In the long run, developing good attention (what's known as *narrowband focus*) pays big dividends when it comes to match play.

2. This game should help you discover your natural strengths and any weaknesses that may need more attention. Try this exercise repeatedly with various shots and see how you perform.

Variation

1. An option in scoring is the loss of 3 points if you hit the designated shot in the net, whereas any other error loses only 2.

The Straight Files

Description

This exercise is the same as "The X Files" except, instead of crosscourt, it's played down the line on either side of the court. The same rules apply (that is, for play to continue down the line until a ball lands short of the service line, at which time the whole court can be used). I suggest playing "The X Files" much more frequently than "The Straight Files" because crosscourt play should be more predominant than down-the-line patterns. But, as a change of pace, "The Straight Files" has its benefits as well.

Helpful Tips

1. Remember that you are hitting over the higher part of the net, and make a conscious decision to hit with great net clearance.
2. In a game like this, you run the risk of becoming complacent and not moving your feet. One option is to recover and touch the center mark on the baseline in between shots. The point is to make the drill as close to a real game situation as possible.

Variations

1. Play this game as "forehands only" or "backhands only" depending on which side of the court you are playing.
2. To discourage hitting into the net, subtract 2 points from the player who hits into the net.
3. You can add the dimension of attacking the net by awarding 2 points any time a player wins a point (after a short ball is hit) from inside the service line.

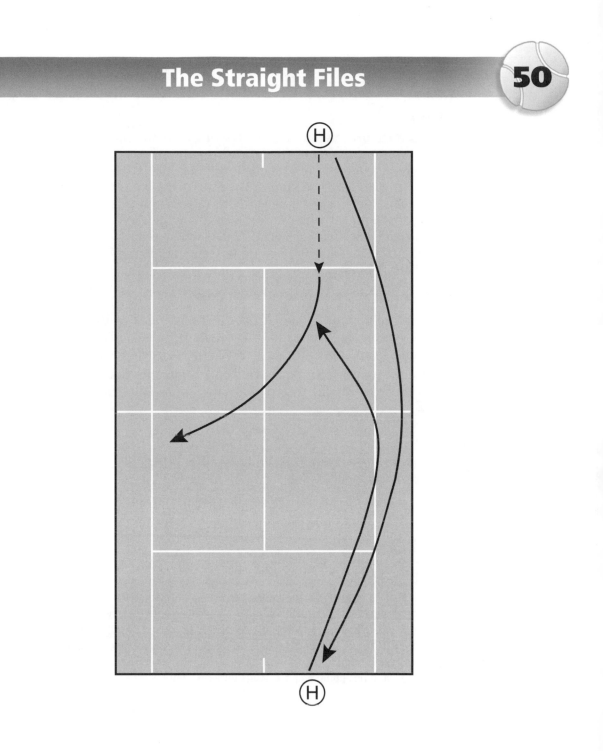

Swing Them Wide

Description

The rules of this next drill encourage you to swing your opponent wide off the court. You and your partner start this game from the baseline with a bounce hit, and whoever hits deep or into the net loses 2 points. If the ball goes wide but not long, you would only lose 1 point. The rules of this game encourage you to hit closer to the sidelines to move your opponent from side to side. It is a great tactic against a player who has trouble moving quickly and recovering from wide balls, and it is effective on clay courts where players have a harder time changing directions quickly because of insecure footing. Play until one player wins 15 or 21 points.

Helpful Tips

1. If you want to focus on groundstrokes without attacking the net, add a rule that you can go to the net only on short balls landing inside the service line. Drop shots are not allowed.

2. If you are the player returning a wide ball, remember that the majority of the time you should return that shot crosscourt to aid in your recovery.

Variations

1. To play this game with serving and normal scoring, take away 2 points in the event of a double fault.

2. Allow each player to hit one ball in each point that lands in the doubles alley.

Did you know?

Many less experienced players think that correct positioning on the baseline means to always recover to the middle of the baseline. On the contrary, you should recover to the middle only when you hit the ball directly down the middle. Otherwise, your baseline position should be diagonally opposite the location where your opponent is striking the ball (assuming he is on the baseline as well). One good way to figure out exactly where you should be is to connect 3 points. Your opponent's contact point is point A. The center T on your side of the net is point B. Your position is point C. Just adjust your position until all 3 points form a straight line.

Freeze

Description

This drill is an enjoyable follow-up to the previous drill. Play with the same rules as in the previous drill, but if you call "freeze" your opponent must stop in her tracks. If you catch her with both feet outside the singles sideline, you win the point immediately. It's not as easy as it sounds, but it's a great drill to develop increased court awareness and a heightened sense of how well you are moving your opponent around on the court. Play until one player wins 15 or 21 points.

Helpful Tips

1. This exercise can help you develop your anticipation skills. If you wait too long to call out "freeze," your opponent may already have recovered back into the court. So, be careful and make sure to call out "freeze" at the right time.

2. If, on the other hand, you are the player whose feet are out of the court, make sure to recover quickly enough not to get caught out of the court. This will help you develop faster recovery skills, a key to successful tennis.

Variations

1. To play this game with serving and normal scoring, take away 2 points in the event of a double fault.

2. More advanced players lose points when both feet of the opponent are outside the doubles sideline.

Did you know?

The singles court is 27 feet wide and the doubles court is 36 feet wide. Considering that the average movement in singles against balls that are hit down the line may be only 50 feet, let's analyze how much more your opponent may have to run if you exclusively hit crosscourt groundstrokes, considering that two side-to-side crosscourt shots can make an opponent run 75 feet. An average set contains 60 points. If, on average, your opponent must move for two shots per point, the extra running against crosscourt shots will be nearly 1,500 feet, almost one-third of a mile. Now ask yourself this: If I can make my opponent run an extra one-third of a mile in each set, should I? You bet you should.

Description

This drill requires the use of rope, chalk, or throw-down rubber lines to extend the singles sidelines from the baseline all the way to the back fence. Start the singles point with a serve down the middle or simply with a bounce-hit groundstroke. After that, anything goes. One of the main strategies in a groundstroke rally is to hit angled shots to move your opponent's feet outside the singles sideline. With the sidelines extended, our players can clearly see what they are trying to accomplish and when they succeed. To create focus, use normal scoring; however, whoever touches or moves outside any part of the new longer singles sideline with one or both feet immediately loses the point.

Helpful Tips

1. One tactical guideline for tennis is to return an angle with an angle because the wider you are (near the sidelines) when you hit a groundstroke, the easier it will be to return that shot with an equal or even sharper angle. The net is lower where the ball will cross, the diagonal is a longer area to hit into, and you are not drastically changing the angle of the incoming ball.

2. As you advance, you should recognize that some footwork patterns are more effective than others, particularly on wide balls. The most efficient way to hit a ball when pulled wide is with an open stance. Although this is particularly true on forehand groundstrokes, it is also common to see open-stance backhands, a maneuver that was practically unheard of a decade ago.

3. If you lay down ropes to extend the lines, make sure to use hollow-braided ropes that sit flat on the court. They are much safer than solid-core ropes, which can roll underfoot.

Variations

1. An alternative to regular scoring is to simply play games until one player wins 11, 15, or 21 points. Still, whoever touches or crosses the extended sideline or the regular one immediately loses the point.

2. This game can be adapted for doubles. In that case, extend the doubles sideline and play with regular scoring or with the rules of the singles variation drill. In doubles, the reason for pulling one player off the court with a well-angled shot is to open up the middle of the court.

Feeling the Net Zone 54

Description

Here's a unique exercise that rapidly improves the kinesthetic awareness, or "feel," for the ball. You'll need a partner who feeds balls from across the net from a position where he can see where the ball lands. You will be visually handicapped because the net has been completely covered by a roll of fabric or paper that you can attach to the net with masking tape. After hitting each ball, tell the feeder where you think the ball landed. At least at the beginning, almost all players will be significantly off in their estimation of where the ball landed. But gradually you should start feeling the ball better off your racket and become accurate in knowing within inches exactly where your balls are landing.

Helpful Tips

1. Rolls of brown or white paper, commonly called butcher paper, are the easiest to use. After a while, however, you will find that balls hitting this paper will tear the paper into many pieces. Test yourself by seeing how long you can use it before it goes to pieces. The longer it lasts, the more balls you are hitting over the net instead of into it.

2. You will notice that the loud popping noise of the balls hitting the net becomes quite a deterrent. It is embarrassing to hit into the net because it can now be heard a block away!

Variations

1. You can play regular-scoring games with serves and returns. Just add the rule that the player who hits the ball into the net immediately loses the game.

2. Give doubles a try as well with the same rules.

Doubles Outside the Middle

Description

For this game you will need four players on the court. First, mark off a middle area of a doubles court by creating a 15-foot-diameter circle with ropes, chalk, or throw-down rubber markers. You will see that the rules of this drill will successfully limit play in doubles to angles only. This middle area becomes the forbidden zone—any balls landing there mean an immediate loss of that point. This type of exercise increases focus on angled shots that players would normally not experience. The result is an expansion of a player's normal repertoire of angled shots. Feel free to adjust the size of the forbidden zone to accommodate different skill levels.

Helpful Tips

1. If you use ropes to mark the area, make sure to use hollow-braided ropes that sit flat on the court because they are much safer than solid-core ropes, which can roll underfoot.

2. We do not suggest using masking tape because it can stick to the courts and may be difficult to remove.

Variation

Remember that the size of the middle area can and should be adjusted to suit players of various skill levels. You can also adjust the size when teams have varying abilities to level the playing field. Just make the middle area of the weaker player smaller than the area of the stronger player.

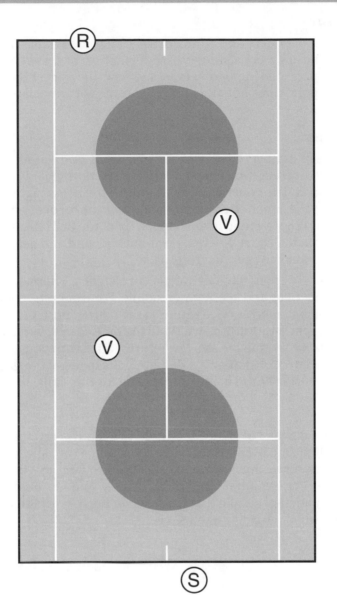

56 Return Cross or Play It Again

Description

This game is cooperative and competitive at the same time. The rules focus on one issue: hitting a consistent crosscourt return of serve in singles. As in normal play, after missing two serves in a row, the server loses the point. However, the point does not start until the return of serve lands crosscourt and in.

Helpful Tips

1. The basic strategy in singles as well as in doubles is to return the majority of serves crosscourt. The five reasons appear in several places in this book: The court diagonal is longer; the net is higher; you are not changing the direction of the incoming ball; the recovery position on the baseline is shorter; and if you happen to hit the ball late, it will probably still land in the court. Keep these points in mind and get yourself to hit mostly crosscourt service returns.

2. This drill is designed to encourage consistency. Therefore, take advantage of the rules and keep things simple. For example, if you usually hit a topspin forehand service return in the deuce court, hit your forehand with topspin in this drill as well—all the time. Don't switch to underspin just because you may miss a few returns. Stick with your game plan and don't deviate. Consistency is definitely the name of the game in tennis, and it is certainly the name of the game for this drill.

Variation

1. Limit the number of returns to three to keep the game going. In other words, if the receiver misses three returns in a row, she loses the point. But if the server misses two serves in a row at any time during the exercise, it is counted as a double fault. And, to help the receiver, consider adding the rule that the receiver must hit the same spin on the returns when returning each serve.

Winning Shot Combinations

An adventurous chef once thought that adding tomatoes to a grilled cheese sandwich would enhance its flavor. And someone thought that a peanut butter sandwich might be tastier with jelly. Anyway, you get the point. Combining ingredients often leads to a better product.

In tennis, we are talking about shot combinations, which fall into two basic categories: transition shots, such as the serve-and-volley or the approach-and-volley combinations; and tactics to vary play and open up the court or to exploit an opponent's weaknesses. For example, you might elect to hit a high-bouncing and deep topspin forehand against a tall player who doesn't like low and short balls; you'd immediately follow this with a short and low backspin ball to force your opponent into an awkward position. The main difference between deploying shot combinations as a tactic versus simply moving from the baseline to the net with a transition stroke such as an approach shot is that your opponent is forced to hit shots he just doesn't like.

Practicing shot combinations, however, poses a challenge for less experienced players. The serve and volley for singles requires a five-shot sequence: the serve, return of serve, first volley from midcourt, return of that first volley, and the final volley fairly close to the net. The problem arises when the return doesn't come back to the server in the first place. In other words, one mistake interrupts the entire five-shot sequence. One solution is to carry extra balls in your pockets. Then, as soon as an error occurs, you can introduce a new ball without starting the entire shot sequence all over again. Otherwise, an advanced beginner might practice for 30 minutes with a partner of comparable ability and never even complete the entire multiple-ball sequence. This is not the ideal way to learn shot combinations.

This chapter is full of creative games to help you practice all types of shot combinations. And, as in the last chapter that featured blocked practice games, the drills in this chapter can be expanded into dozens of variations, one for each situation in the game. After you isolate a particular set of skills or game situation you need to practice, create a specific drill designed to meet your needs.

Patterns of play and shot combinations are more important on the women's pro tour than on the men's tour because points consistently last longer.

Description

Beginners or even intermediate-level players learn to serve and volley or chip and charge, and they do just that: charge, full steam ahead. Sometimes the problem is not so much getting to the net as getting there without crashing into it—either the players themselves or the balls they just hit. Even if you don't have this specific problem, this drill is still worth a try. Instead of running to the net, try walking. It's similar to getting kids to walk in school corridors—the result is a lot more control and balance. Play regular games of doubles with the following rules: Poaching is not allowed, and the receiver cannot charge the net or lob the returns. Once the server is halfway between the service line and the net, anything goes and players can resume running.

Helpful Tips

1. Even though you are walking, remember to split step.

2. At first this exercise will seem awkward and it will be hard to hold yourself back from running. Hang in there; it is an experience that is well worth the effort.

3. After four games of walking to the net, try it full speed. If successful, keep going. If not, try walking for another four games until running works comfortably.

Variations

1. To get an initial feel for this exercise, don't play full points. Rather, let each player try it four times and just try to perform a cooperative five-shot sequence (as explained in the introduction to this chapter).

2. This exercise is also helpful for singles. And, although you will have to cover more court area, remember that it is just as important to be on balance in singles as it is in doubles.

3. For less advanced players, also consider starting this drill with the server serving from the service line to increase the number of volley opportunities.

Issue Focus Drills

Description

Experts agree that narrow-band focus is good for tennis. This exercise helps you concentrate on one particular shot combination (for example, an approach and volley or returning serve with a chip and charge). The opposite is to have players try to concentrate all the time. The typical result of trying to concentrate all the time is regular lapses in focus. The other benefit of isolating particular focus issues is to get players more in the moment. Play games to 11, 15, 21, or regular sets; and award 2 points for all points won by coming to the net since this is the focus.

Helpful Tips

1. You'll probably benefit greatly from watching top-flight players compete. Go to local college matches and evaluate when the players are focusing well and when they are not. You could also tape world-class tennis matches on television and replay the most exciting portions. Practice your own focus by putting yourself in a player's shoes.

2. Bring a piece of paper to your own matches and, in between games, mark how you would evaluate your focus on a scale of 1 to 10.

Variations

The variations of this concept are endless. Just pick a specific focus issue and keep concentrating on that one thing in the midst of playing a regular set of tennis. Also consider other focus issues such as concentrating on hitting a certain type of spin, arc over the net, direction, or depth.

Did you know?

Studies have established that the average human being has roughly 50,000 different thoughts a day. With that in mind, you'll find it easy to understand why most players find focusing on a tennis court one of the most basic yet most challenging aspects of successful play. To help players improve their concentration, instructors have long called out, "Watch the ball" as a way to help the players create a more narrow focus and concentrate more on the object they are supposed to be tracking. The device you select to help your concentration doesn't really matter. What does matter is that your focus improves as quickly as your skill improves. Otherwise, you will just be one more tennis player others describe as "She sure looks good on the court, but she just can't win a match."

Description

There's one drill we've all seen again and again. One player feeds to another player at the net who alternates between volleys and overhead smashes. Here's a variation that fits perfectly into the concept of practicing shot combinations in a game-based environment. However, instead of alternating volleys and regular overheads, try alternating volleys and backhand overheads. The backhand overhead is a difficult shot, yet it is seldom practiced. It's one shot that, when executed properly, can win points and increase self-confidence tremendously. But when it's executed poorly, it's a good way to lose confidence and the momentum needed to succeed. You will need a practice partner for this drill. One of you feeds a volley and then a lob over the backhand side to the other player. The point starts when the backhand overhead is hit successfully into the court. This is a fairly tough drill, so just play first to reach 5 points and then switch roles.

Helpful Tip

Because the backhand overhead is such a tough shot, allow the person who is going to hit it to reject the feed if it is just too difficult. At many levels, it just doesn't make sense to go after shots that may be just too tough to retrieve. As you build your confidence, try tougher and tougher shots.

Variation

To adjust this game for doubles, four players can compete as follows: Two start at the baseline and feed an initial ball to the team at the net who volley it back to the baseliners with control. The baseliners then lob the ball over the backhand side of one of the volleyers. As soon as a backhand overhead is successfully hit, the point is played out. Play first team to reach 7 points and then rotate sides.

True Story

The 2001 U.S. Open quarterfinal match between Andre Agassi and Pete Sampras will stand out in tennis history as one of the most exciting matches of all time. Sampras won 6-7, 7-6, 7-6, 7-6. In the critical second-set tiebreak, Pete hit a backhand overhead winner, perfectly angled and impossible to return, even for Agassi. It was clear that Sampras' confidence soared and Agassi wondered how he could win if Pete continued to play at that high level.

60 Seesaw

Description

This is a cooperative drill with continuous scoring that uses the service lines to divide each side of the court between short and long. Hitting baseline to baseline with a practice partner, you score 1 positive point as a team for each ball that lands in the court behind the service line and 1 negative point for each ball landing short, in the net, out of play, or not returned. If an error occurs, just feed another ball to continue the drill and continue scoring from where you left off. Count out loud with every shot you both hit and see how quickly as a pair you can reach 21 points. Then, when you reach 21, play out that last point competitively, with either player approaching the net on the next short ball. If there is no short ball hit, the player who loses that last point feeds a ball short to allow the player on the other side of the net to hit an approach-and-volley shot combination.

Helpful Tips

1. This is a good example of a drill whose rules guide effective on-court technical behavior. You want to be steady at the baseline and realize that short balls generally come with a penalty—that your opponent will come to the net and dictate play.
2. Remember to simply increase the arc of the ball over the net to keep most balls deep.
3. The main challenge of this drill is to score loudly enough to keep both you and your partner focused.

Variations

1. Turn this exercise into a competitive drill by having both players call their individual score out loud.
2. The exercise can also be performed with four players hitting one ball. In that case, the team members on each side of the net alternate hits.
3. For extra fitness, try variation number 2 but, in between shots, each player must run back and touch the back fence. This will aid in developing good recovery timing as well, because the players will not have a moment to stand around and admire the shot they just hit.

Strategy

Players hear all the time that, in singles, you should come to the net as often as possible, especially when your opponent's ball lands short. But what does short mean? Inexperienced players tend to think that when the ball lands inside the service line on their side of the net, it is short enough for them to come to the net. Although often true, this is not always the case. Let your court position determine whether you will come to the net. If your feet are on or behind the baseline, usually you should stay back. But if your feet are well inside the baseline when you contact the ball, treat it as a welcome mat saying, "Come on in!"

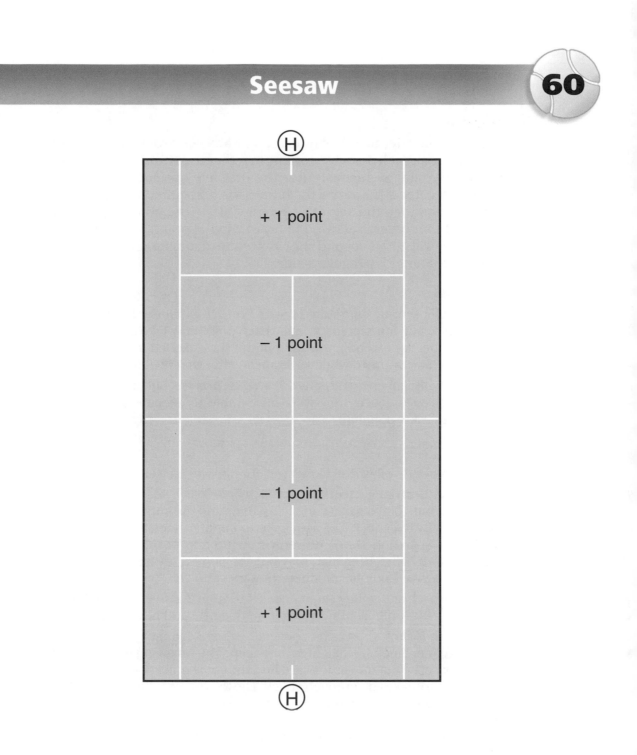

61 Cooperative Serve and Volley

Description

This exercise simulates match play in a cooperative environment. You and your partner begin each point by working together to control an initial five-ball serve-and-volley sequence. After the first five specific shots in sequence are executed—the serve, the return, the first volley, the receiver's second shot, and then the server's second volley—the point begins. On this fifth shot the server is allowed to try to win the point. Therefore, the smart receiver will hit his second shot low to the incoming server's feet to neutralize the point. Play regular games.

Helpful Tips

1. Play regular scoring but rotate servers every five minutes if the game in progress is not completed, because each point may take a while to get started, thereby extending the amount of time needed for each game. Just award the game to whoever is ahead after that five-minute period.

2. This drill will challenge the patience of some players, but unless you can control this sequence, how will you be able to execute serving and volleying in a real match?

Variations

1. This serve-and-volley drill works well for doubles as well as for singles.

2. Expand this strategy to the approach-and-volley sequence. In that situation, both players start on the baseline and the initial bounce hit is intentionally fed short. The sequence to initiate the point is the short feed, the approach shot, the return of the approach, and then the volley—four balls. After that, play out the point. Play games until one player reaches 7 points, and then rotate positions.

3. The approach-and-volley sequence in variation 2 also works well with four players. Apply all other rules from this drill and have fun!

4. Try the four-shot approach-volley-and-volley sequence. In this case, one baseliner feeds the ball high and deep. The receiving player starts on the baseline but moves forward into the court quickly as soon as the feed is hit to make an approach volley. The third shot is the return of the approach volley, and by then the attacking player has moved in for the fourth shot, an attempt at a winning volley from a position well inside the service line. All other rules as previously explained apply.

Description

For this exercise you will need four players. It's a doubles drill that encourages the serving team to take charge of the net quickly. At the same time the receiving team is forced to concentrate on keeping the returns low at the incoming server's feet to force her into a defensive position. If the return of serve bounces on the server's side before either member of the serving team can hit the volley, the receiving team wins the point. No lobs are allowed on the return of serve. The result is a very focused and competitive atmosphere with a lot of movement because poaching is a tactic that the serving team will want to employ frequently. The shot combination is to hit a drop return of serve to force the serving team to volley up and then for the receiving team to take over the net and volley the ball away for a winner.

Helpful Tips

1. We all know that service returns are best hit with small backswings. This drill will help the receivers with this technique, because a large backswing will not yield winning results in this exercise.

2. Occasionally, players will try to hit the service returns with topspin. Although this is an effective way to get balls to dip at the incoming server's feet, It can also be inconsistent because of the difficult timing involved in brushing up enough on the return to create sufficient topspin. Start chipping or blocking the returns and then, once you master that skill, try to move on to topspin.

Variations

1. Have each player serve just 4 points to the deuce court and rotate all players through that position. Then, shift to the ad court and rotate the same way.

2. Instead of regular scoring, just have each player serve 4 points per game. If it reaches 2-all, play a fifth and final point to see which team wins that game.

Strategy

The rules of this game raise the question of power versus control. Because the shift in the world of topflight tennis is toward increasing power and speed, the general playing public often thinks that today's world-class players are hitting with all power and little or no finesse. It is true that the best players hit with more force than ever before, but they are also masters of control and finesse. When a match is over, it reads 6-1, 6-3. There are no footnotes saying that although you lost, you hit with tremendous power.

Description

We all know that as players advance they must gradually perfect shot sequences. After all, one of the sport's biggest attractions is the excitement that only an open sport like tennis can create. In contrast, closed sports such as track, swimming, or even golf are very different. They don't provide the same head-to-head competitive excitement with the unexpected happening all the time. However, at advanced beginner and intermediate levels, when players begin learning shot combinations, these random game situations can be challenging. Players make mistakes and become frustrated. The concept of this drill meets this challenge. All you need is tennis clothing with big pockets to comfortably hold a few balls. Let's say that you and a partner are trying to practice a five-shot serve-and-volley sequence for singles. In normal practice most attempts at this full sequence tend to fail because one of you makes a mistake. A positive option is to try it this way: As soon as one of you misses a shot in the sequence, instead of heading back to the baseline to start over, continue the pattern immediately without interruption by grabbing a ball from your pocket and continuing right where you left off. This way, each attempt at the five-ball sequence is completed. This guarantees that you will keep the goal clearly in mind and be encouraged to continue practicing.

Helpful Tips

1. Players should begin each sequence with at least two or three balls in their pockets.
2. Players can execute this concept in two ways. One way is for the player who made the error to replay that same shot. The other option is for the player on the other side of the net to pretend that the ball was kept in play, and bounce and hit a ball from his pocket to continue the sequence as if no mistake occurred. Try it both ways and see which system suits you best.

Variations

This concept works well for all shot sequences. Here are several examples:

1. Serve and volley
2. Chip and charge
3. Approach and volley
4. Approach, volley, and volley

Decisive Shot Selection

Once you can execute the basic shots of tennis, the next requirement for hitting any tennis ball is making the decision where to hit it. It sounds basic, but it really isn't.

At the 1996 U.S. Open, tour player and former collegiate star Scott Humphries was playing a tough early-round match. At a critical point toward the end of the second set, Scott's opponent hit a short, high "sitter," exactly what Scott would have hoped for. The ball bounced just inside the service line. Scott moved in to put the ball away and win the point to break serve.

Unfortunately, he hit the ball out of the court. Scott screamed, "Make up your mind!"

A few years later I ran into Scott's former college coach in an airport, and we started talking about Scott, who had been recognized as one of the most talented players in the United States for a long time. Scott had the ability to hit a variety of shots on any given ball. Unlike many players, Scott could take a high-bouncing sitter and hit it with power to the corners or turn it into a deadly drop shot. Unfortunately, Scott had too many choices and often had trouble deciding which shot to hit. In that ill-fated moment at the U.S. Open, Scott's talent turned against him. He had too many choices and couldn't make up his mind. After missing the shot he became so disappointed in himself that he went on to lose the match.

This chapter features a series of decision-making drills designed to help players of all levels become more decisive and therefore more effective. The rules of the various games and exercises will train you to make quick decisions, sometimes based simply on percentage tennis and sometimes just on your personal preferences. As in many of the chapters in this book, the rules of the individual drill will guide your on-court habits toward improved levels of play.

The principle of having only two choices is called *binary focus*. The advice for tennis players at most levels is to keep shot selection simple and to be as consistent as possible; this is what wins matches. In other words, don't make a fairly complex sport more complicated. Narrow down your choices to one or two options and be decisive about what you intend to do.

Lindsay Davenport's shotmaking is always decisive when she is playing well.

Description

In this drill you and a practice partner stand on opposite baselines while one feeds a variety of shots to the other. The object is for the hitter to call out 1, 2, or 3 as the ball crosses the net. Number 1 means the hitter is in a defensive position and will aim for depth, consistency, and good net clearance. Number 2 means the player will try to pressure the opponent with direction, depth, and moderate pace. Number 3 means that the player will try to hit a winner. Feed 10 balls and rotate positions. The result of practicing this exercise is consistency with fewer unforced errors, the natural result of early decision making.

Helpful Tips

1. Isolate one shot at a time if necessary. In other words, instead of feeding a variety of balls, concentrate on one particular situation at a time. Then, once you have mastered that skill, move on from there to create a more random practice environment.

2. The key to this drill is early decision making. Therefore, challenge yourself by trying to call out the appropriate number well in advance. Remember to call it out loudly, clearly, and confidently. It makes a difference.

Variations

1. You can adjust this concept by decreasing this drill to two numbers of your choice to make it simpler for less advanced players.

2. With three players this drill works just as well. Appoint the third player as the "coach" to stand behind one of the players. It is then the coach's responsibility to call out the numbers for the player on the same side of the net; this adds more objectivity to the exercise.

65 Color Ball

Description

Generally speaking, the decision of what shot to attempt is up to you as the hitter. At the same time, many situations also force just one sensible shot dictated by the ball your opponent just hit. To play this game you need a bucket with two different-colored balls and either a person feeding to you or a ball machine feeding to you. Then, assign each color a different type of shot. For example, if you have yellow balls and orange balls, hit all yellow balls down the line and hit all orange balls crosscourt. To create a game with several players, simply assign 1 point for each ball hit into the correct area and give each player five feeds in a row before rotating. The first player to reach 21 points wins the game.

Helpful Tips

1. This drill is one of those ideas that can be turned into hundreds of different drills. Just a few are listed in the variations.

2. In each case, remember that it is generally best to have only two choices.

Variations

1. Use drop shots or approach shots.

2. Use topspin or backspin groundstrokes.

3. Use drop shots either crosscourt or down the line.

4. Use flat groundstrokes or looping groundstrokes with topspin.

5. Use topspin lobs or backspin (defensive) lobs.

6. On short balls, two choices are to hit an approach shot or to try to hit a winner.

7. At the net, use volleys or drop volleys.

8. At the net, use volleys or lob volleys.

9. Use overheads crosscourt or down the line.

10. Use passing shots down the line or crosscourt.

11. For players hitting backhands with two hands, hit with two hands or one depending on the incoming ball.

Description

A consistent return of serve is one of the keys to successful tennis, and the return of serve is also one of the most challenging shots in the game (see "Did you know?" on page 46). It requires split-second judgment and preparation. If you are returning serve, you must decide *before* the server even contacts the ball what you will do if the serve is hit to your forehand and what you will do if it comes to your backhand. This is exactly what you will attempt in this drill. Well before the server contacts the ball, the receiver has to commit where to hit the return and call out loud the two choices (one for the backhand and one for the forehand) from the following list:

- Forehand down the line
- Forehand crosscourt
- Backhand down the line
- Backhand crosscourt

If the return of serve lands in the announced half of the court, the point is played out. If it doesn't land in the announced half, the receiver gets two more chances to succeed. However, after three errors in a row, the point is lost. From the server's perspective, double faults do not count. The server just keeps going until the serve goes in. When it does go in, the server waits for the return to land in the proper half of the court to begin the point.

Helpful Tips

1. The server should not start serving until the receiver clearly calls out the intended returns.
2. The callout allows the server to start planning what to do with her next shot as well, which is another important ingredient of winning tennis.

Variations

1. Chip and charge either with a down-the-line approach, a crosscourt short-angled approach, or a drop shot.
2. Attack the net behind a crosscourt or down-the-line drive.
3. Have the server come in behind the serve. Then counterpunch low to the feet of a server and volleyer, calling out in advance either, "Crosscourt," or "Down the line."
4. Hit a runaround forehand either crosscourt or down the line.

Thirds

Description

For this two-player baseline exercise, divide the width of the singles court into thirds with flat ropes or rubber throw-down lines. Start each point with a bounce hit from the middle third on one side and hit into the middle third on the other side of the net. After that, anything goes; but before hitting each ball, each player must call out whether it will be hit in the middle third of the court, crosscourt on an angle to pull their opponent's feet outside the singles sideline, or deep down the line. If the ball misses the intended target, the point is lost. Games are played until one player reaches 15 points.

Helpful Tips

1. Note that flat or hollow-braided ropes are safer than normal solid-braided round ropes that can roll underfoot.
2. If this drill is too difficult to execute in the full singles court, less experienced players move forward to play within the service boxes.

Variations

1. Divide the court into thirds with ropes or lines on only one side of the court. One person plays with the "thirds" rule and the opposing player can hit into the open court as desired. If you wish, play to 11 points but start the game with the player hitting into the "thirds" with a 7-0 lead.
2. Add the rule that the player who has the ropes or rubber lines on her side must move to the third of the court called out by the hitter before that ball lands on the "thirds" side of the net. This will help the player develop early preparation and good movement skills. This may not be as easy as it sounds, but give it a try.
3. Play the "thirds," but divide up the doubles court instead of just the singles court. Although using the alleys for singles is an exaggeration, the exercise will encourage players to hit with greater angles when they return to using just the singles court.
4. Play variation 3, but only balls that land in the alleys short of the service lines on both sides are good. This encourages even greater angles.

Did you know?

A singles tennis court is 27 feet wide. Divide it in thirds and you end up with 9 feet for each third. A doubles court is 36 feet wide. Divide it into thirds and each section is 12 feet wide. The doubles alley is 4.5 feet wide.

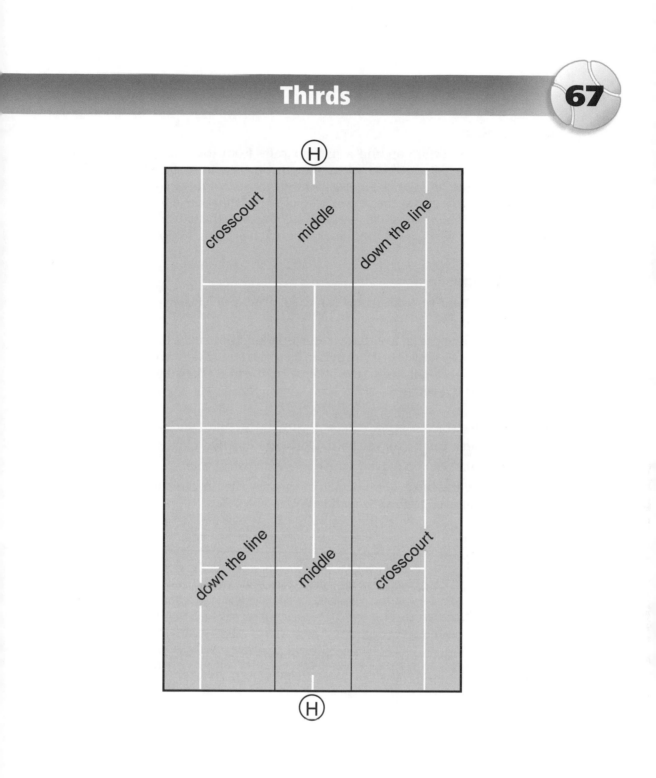

In to the Net

Description

In this decision drill, you and a partner rally from the baseline against a competing team. After a three-ball exchange from baseline to baseline, anyone can call out loud "in," which signals that the team is coming in behind a short ball. The only rule is that the person who calls "in" must have both feet inside the baseline. He should call "in" early enough—before the ball crosses onto his side of the net. Play games until one team reaches 11 or 15 points, and then change sides.

Helpful Tips

1. Remember that both teams can call "in" to move their teams in to the net.
2. It is a good idea to alternate teams that feed the initial ball that keep it fair for both sides. Or, if you prefer, have the team that won the last point feed the next ball to give the other team the first chance to call "in" and come to the net.

Variations

1. This game can be played as singles with only two players.
2. This game can be played as two players against one.
3. You can add the rule that when one team calls "in," the opposing team is not allowed to lob the next ball.

Strategy

Although it has been around for years, the strategic concept called the *stoplight theory* is still worth mentioning for beginning- through intermediate-level players. Think of the tennis court in terms of a traffic light. If your feet are behind the baseline when you contact the ball, you are in the red zone. If your feet are in front of the baseline but not more than halfway to the service line when you contact the ball, you are in the yellow zone. If your feet are anywhere in front of the yellow zone when you contact the ball, you are in the green zone. After that it's simple. Red zone, stay back. Green zone, go to the net without hesitation. Yellow zone, you have a decision to make depending on factors such as your style of play and how well your opponent hits passing shots.

Description

This vision-training and anticipation baseline drill requires two players rallying from baseline to baseline; however, each side of the singles court is divided into four quadrants designated one through four. They consist of the two service boxes and the two halves of the backcourt area. Just extend the center service line with chalk, string, flat ropes, or rubber throw-down lines. Start each point with a bounce hit from the baseline with each of you calling out the number of the quadrant you think each shot will land as or before the ball crosses the net. The initial feed must be aimed toward one of the deep two quadrants, but after that anything goes. The winner of each point feeds the next point, and games are played until one player reaches 11 or 15 points. Points are immediately lost if the ball does not land in the quadrant called out by the hitter.

Helpful Tips

1. If you use ropes, use the flat or hollow-braided kind instead of solid-braided round ropes that can roll underfoot if stepped on.
2. If this drill is too difficult initially, less experienced players can adjust the rules to play within the service boxes. But in this event, remember to divide the area into four sections and number the quadrants. Then, as quickly as possible, move back to the full-court area.

Variations

1. Divide the court into four quadrants on one side only. One player will have to play with the "quadrants" rule of calling out intent, and the opposing player can hit into the open court as desired. If you wish, play to 11 points but start the game with the player hitting into the "quadrants" with a 7-0 lead.
2. Add the doubles alleys and number the alleys as 5 and 6 to create more movement and a more challenging drill.
3. Add the doubles alleys but only require the players to call out "alley" before the shot crosses the net. This challenges the opposing player to be attentive. Although this may sound unfair to the receiving player, remember that if "alley" is called but the ball does not land in the alley, the point is immediately lost. Plus, although using the alleys for singles is an exaggeration, the exercise encourages players to hit with greater angles after they return to using just the singles court.
4. Play variation 3, but the "alley" balls are good only if they land short of the service lines on both sides. This encourages even greater angles.

The Shadow

Description

This exercise requires three players. Two of you hit from baseline to baseline, and the third player is behind one of you along the back fence. This third player acts as the "shadow" of the player in front of him; however, this shadow actually moves before the person in front does. Immediately after the player on the same side of the net hits the ball, the shadow player calls out loud "right" or "left" to the player in front of him while simultaneously moving along the fence toward the singles sideline in the direction indicated. The hitting player on the side of the shadow has to move to and touch the same singles sideline. The winner of each point bounce hits the next ball. As soon as one player wins 5 points, the players rotate positions. The player opposite the shadow is not allowed to hit drop shots, and the player on the same side of the shadow is not allowed to come to the net.

Helpful Tips

1. You will quickly see that for this exercise to work smoothly, the shadow must move and call out the direction immediately after the player on the same side contacts the ball.

2. Play this game diligently with the shadow sprinting along the fence to the sideline in the direction called out. The added conditioning benefits of moving quickly will pay big dividends in real match play.

3. Make sure the singles player (opposite the shadow) does not become compassionate and hit to the same side the opposing players have moved. Get in the habit of exploiting obvious weaknesses.

Variations

1. You can allow drop shots with the shadow's partner coming to the net. In that event, the shadow takes a break and the other two players finish the point.

2. Add a bonus point to the scoring system if the player without the shadow hits a clean winner (untouched by the opposing player) on the side opposite where the shadow has run.

3. Add a bonus point to the scoring system if the player opposite the shadow hits *behind* the player (in other words, toward the singles sideline she has just touched and is running from).

Description

The serve is the most important shot in tennis. It begins each point, and more serves are hit than any other shot in every single match. This exercise helps you identify your options when serving and practice the all-important decision of which type of serve to hit where. It may sound simple, but it really isn't because at least 18 options exist in both service boxes. When you consider that you have three basic types of serves (flat, slice, or kick) and three directions that can be hit toward (wide, at the body, or down the middle of the court), each service box has nine options. The drill is for you to practice serving, either alone or with a partner, and to call out your intentions before hitting the serve.

Helpful Tips

1. Although it may seem unnecessary, calling your intent out loud is significant because it helps firm up your decision-making habits, a very important part of becoming a better server.

2. After calling out your intent, pause a second or two before actually hitting the serve to visualize it as well.

Variations

1. To increase your concentration if you are practicing alone, keep track of your serves in increments of 10 to understand your percentage of success; in this sense, success means hitting the ball in the direction and manner you planned.

2. With a partner, you can create a little friendly competition by alternating serving and judging each other, keeping track of your percentages.

3. If you are alone on a court, you can play a set against yourself by counting a successful serve as a point won. Then go to the next box and keep playing with regular scoring. The only difference from regular play is that you will serve all the games, and you should allow only one serve per point.

Training and Match Strategy

Perception and Anticipation

Consider this comparison of returning a serve in tennis to reacting to a pitch in baseball: In baseball, the distance between the pitcher and the batter is 90 feet. In tennis, the diagonal distance between the server and the receiver is slightly more than 80 feet. A 90-mile-per-hour fastball travels from the pitcher's hand to the batter in 1.5 seconds. Out of that time frame, you need at least one-quarter of a second to see the ball, send the image to the brain, and decide how to swing. This means that in professional baseball, the best batters decide whether to swing when the pitch is only 15 to 20 feet from the mound. It gets even more complex when curve balls, breaking balls, and sliders are thrown—pitches that move unpredictably as they approach the batter.

Because a tennis ball loses half its speed after it bounces (a 90-mile-per-hour serve will slow to 45 miles per hour after the bounce), the equation in rounded figures gives the receiver closer to 1.75 seconds between the time the server hits and the time the receiver contacts the ball. But in tennis, two major complications exist. First, the strike zone in tennis is huge compared to the zone in baseball because the service box is 21 by 18 feet. Second, the ball has to be hit on both sides of the body with either a forehand or backhand, whereas in baseball the batter waits with his bat in a prepared

Anna Kournikova has won more than her share of doubles titles. She obviously has terrific perception and anticipation skills.

position. In other words, in tennis the receiver must make bigger decisions and take the time to prepare more than in baseball. The bottom line is that returning serves (or any shot, for that matter) is challenging and requires all the perception and anticipation skills you can muster.

Tennis is an open sport that contains an infinite number of variables on every shot. The key to tennis lies in preparation—being at the right place at the right time to strike the incoming ball. If you are in the wrong place or swing the racket at the wrong time, you're doomed to fail, or at least make a lot of mistakes.

Getting in correct position within the fraction of a second needed to hit a tennis ball requires a head start. That head start is called *anticipation*—knowing where you are going to hit the ball before you strike it or immediately after contact. Good anticipation requires good perception. This chapter contains games and drills to help you develop those critical skills. In tennis, time is the issue. Prepare early and you'll be a better player, no matter whether you are already on the pro tour or just starting and learning how to keep score.

Description

One of the first concerns in playing tennis is to know whether your opponent is going to hit the ball powerfully or softly. A slow-looping groundstroke can take up to three seconds to travel from baseline to baseline; a power groundstroke takes as little as one second or less. In this cooperative exercise you and your partner will hit random groundstrokes slowly or powerfully. The player opposite the person hitting the ball calls out "slow" or "fast" *before* every ball is hit (or as soon after contact as possible) based on how he perceives the ball has been hit. Generally speaking, the size of the backswing tells the story: The bigger the backswing, the more power to expect.

Helpful Tips

1. Advanced players will be better able than beginners to disguise their shots (that is, they will be able to take a similar backswing for both shots hit with power or with less pace). Although this is a relatively advanced concept, even advanced beginners can begin heading in that direction.

2. To begin developing disguise, you may want to feed balls to one another while the feeder calls out to the hitter "slow" or "fast" at the last second. This will force the hitter to change ball speed by varying the speed of the forward swing while keeping a similar backswing.

Variations

1. Adjust the drill for direction. Call out, "Down the line" or "Crosscourt" before your partner hits the ball.

2. Adjust the drill for spin. Call out "backspin" or "topspin" before your partner hits the ball.

3. Adjust the drill for lobs and passing shots. Feed from the volley position at the net and call out "lob" or "passing shot" before or as your partner hits the ball, based on what you perceive is coming.

4. Adjust the drill for disguised drop shots. Feed from the baseline and call out "groundstroke" or "drop shot" just before or as your partner hits the ball. Note that the feed should bring the hitter inside the baseline where it is practical to attempt a drop shot (as opposed to behind the baseline, where a drop shot is considered a low-percentage shot and is easy to chase down).

Balls on the Rise

Description

Today's fast-paced tennis dictates that players take balls earlier and earlier. You will even see this style of play on clay courts, which traditionally encouraged players to stay well behind the baseline. This new style of play allows you to rush your opponent as well as increase your possible angles of play. This exercise will speed up your anticipation skills by forcing you to hit the ball earlier than normal. You will have no choice but to move earlier and faster if you want to stay competitive in this game. The simple rule of play in this game is that after the serve, both players must stay within the singles court. Either player who steps on or behind the baseline or singles sidelines loses the point. You might immediately think, *That's fine. I'll just go to the net.* But beware: In this game lobs quickly become winners if you let them bounce, because you can't run outside the singles court to retrieve them!

Helpful Tips

1. Hitting down the middle will minimize the angles your opponent will be able to hit.

2. It's a good idea to minimize your backswing because you will have less time to react and prepare. Taking the balls on the rise also means they will have more speed; therefore, you will need less backswing to generate power.

Variations

1. Play the same game with four players inside the doubles court.

2. Set up a rope three feet behind the baseline, allowing the players to move outside the sidelines but not behind the rope. (For safety, use ropes that lie flat or are hollow braided.)

Finger Tennis

Description

In this unique cooperative exercise, you and a partner rally from baseline to baseline. One player is assigned the task of holding up one to five fingers of the nonracket hand immediately after hitting each shot. The opposing player has to call out the number of fingers held up before he returns the shot just hit. This will help you get accustomed to observing your opponent more closely before hitting each shot. The benefit is that if the opponent is out of position, you should become more aware and hit to the most strategically advantageous part of the court.

Helpful Tips

1. The key to the success of this cooperative drill is for the designated finger-pointing player to hold up a certain number of fingers as quickly as possible after striking each shot, definitely before the ball she just hit clears the net.

2. At first you may feel challenged by this exercise and perhaps even feel distracted. But stick with it because the subtle and not-so-subtle rewards can be significant.

Variations

1. Have the hitter call out a number from one to five, and the receiver has to repeat it. This increases your attention to hearing, which helps you to discern when spin is placed on the ball and to listen for mis-hits.

2. You can play this drill with both players putting up fingers and calling out the numbers.

Cover the Net to Play a Set

Description

Here's a training idea that develops perception skills on many levels. You will need to cover the net with some type of material: a sheet, blanket, or brown packing paper and masking tape. The effect is twofold. First, it forces players to increase their feel for the ball because they can no longer see where it bounces. Second, this exercise takes away that split-second pause that so often occurs when players stand still to watch where their balls will land instead of recover for their next shot. Find a partner and alternate feeding to each other. Hit groundstrokes and aim for different areas of the court, calling out both the direction of the ball and whether it landed behind or in front of the service line. After the ball lands, the feeder should correct the hitter as needed based on where the ball actually landed. Rotate after 10 feeds.

Helpful Tips

1. Brown paper on a roll is readily available, and with a little masking tape it works well for this drill. There's no way to hide that the ball was hit into the net because you'll hear a wonderfully loud "pop!" The down side, of course, is that paper will tear. Expect the paper to last at least an hour of drilling, depending on how many balls you hit into the net.

2. Covering the net works well indoors all the time but outdoors only on days with little wind.

Variations

1. Have the hitter call out exactly where he thought the ball landed (for example, 10 feet inside the baseline and 5 feet inside the singles sideline).

2. Cover the net for a great addition to a social tournament. This helps cool things down if play ever starts heating up with two players challenging each other's line calls. Because they would no longer be able to see where their balls are landing, they would either have to learn to trust each other or find a new opponent!

3. Perform the variations with the serve.

Description

The serve is the most important shot in tennis. But the return of serve is a close second. The major concern in returning serve is to know what's coming: Is it fast or slow; to your forehand, backhand, or at the body; or hit with spin or flat? One giveaway is recognizing a pattern (for example, all first serves are hard and flat and all second serves have a slice). Sometimes the placement of the toss also announces what kind of serve is coming. A ball tossed out in front can often telegraph a flat serve, and a right-handed server's toss far to the right can announce a slice serve is on the way. The primary drill is for you and your partner to alternate serving 10 balls to each service box. The receiver calls out "A," "B," or "C" as soon as possible after the server contacts the ball. "A" is for balls that will land close to the doubles alley. "B" is for balls that are down the middle of the box, toward the body. "C" is for balls that go down the center of the court, close to the center service line. Just see how early you can call out the letters and how accurate you are with your calls.

Helpful Tips

1. As players advance, they will be able to disguise their serves better and better. This means that they will be able to toss the ball in almost the same place and still be able to vary the direction, spin, and speed of their serves. Although this is an advanced concept, even advanced beginners should gradually start developing this skill.

2. To begin developing disguise, you may want to pair up with another player. The one not serving calls out "A," "B," or "C" just after the server releases the toss. The server then aims for those targets as explained previously. This forces the server to vary the serves by working his racket head angle and speed instead of trying to vary his toss.

Variations

1. Adjust the drill for spin. The receiver calls out "slice" or "flat" (add "topspin" or "kick" for advanced players) as soon as possible after the server hits the ball.

2. Adjust the drill for spin and direction by having the receiver call out "slice middle" or "flat wide" as soon as possible after the server hits the ball.

Comfort Zones

Description

This exercise confronts the complex skills of proper positioning to hit groundstrokes. Rally with a partner from baseline to baseline; as each of you contacts the ball, or just after, call out how your body position was relative to what would make you feel most comfortable. For example, call out "too close" or "too far" or "too high" to describe a relatively bad position to the ball. If you are in ideal position, call out, "Great!" A result of this simple exercise will be increased footwork to get into proper position and an automatic effort to increase your perception and anticipation skills for judging the incoming ball and moving more quickly into position.

Helpful Tips

1. Call out loudly and clearly. This has two purposes: First, enthusiasm is contagious. Second, your own skills will improve more rapidly if you hear yourself describe your position.

2. Remember that the exercise is cooperative. This means that both of you should hit the ball solidly but consistently to take advantage of the rules of this drill.

Variations

1. Instead of rallying in the entire singles court, you can also isolate each groundstroke by hitting balls only crosscourt in each direction. But remember to recover toward the middle after each hit to keep yourself moving correctly.

2. To add a competitive ingredient, hit four balls back and forth cooperatively and then play out the point, still calling out descriptions as explained previously in this exercise.

3. The variations can also be transferred to a doubles drill: Have four players rally from the baseline with no drop shots allowed.

Strategy

This exercise leads us to recognize what types of groundstrokes players like and don't like. Ask yourself three questions about your opponents: Do they like to hit balls that are close to their bodies or far away? Do they like to hit balls that are high or low? Do they like balls that are fast or slow? Once you have your answers, your job is to give them balls they don't like. This is the basic strategy of winning tennis.

Feed a few balls in the warm-up and watch what happens. Feed a slow ball down the middle and, if your opponent moves around the forehand to hit a backhand, right away you know you're playing someone who is scared to hit a forehand. If she moves into position to hit her groundstrokes far away from her body, jam her in the match. If she likes taking it high, keep it low. Look at the next drill and table for more on this pattern of thought.

Description

This chapter would not be complete without discussing the importance of perceiving mechanical stroke limitations as a way to significantly help your anticipation skills. This exercise is not an active drill like the others in this chapter; however, it is just as important as any of them. Knowing that a player has a stroke style that limits him to hit a ball with a certain spin or in a certain direction can give you the edge you need in competition. Review the following chart. Then observe some of your peers; you will quickly see the value of being able to spontaneously recognize these self-limiting techniques.

Mechanical Strokes

Description	Limitation	Ways to Exploit
Hits a particular groundstroke with the lead heel off the ground in a consistent pattern.	Nervousness with that groundstroke.	Hit balls to that side, especially on important, pressure-packed points.
Hits forehand groundstroke with a full Western grip.	Trouble with low balls, especially when near the net.	Hit low short balls with backspin to the forehand side.
Hits forehand groundstroke with a continental grip.	Trouble with high balls.	Hit high-looping, topspin groundstrokes to the forehand side.
Hits serve with "frying pan," or Western grip.	Hits flat first serves and weak second serves with no spin.	Move in on slow second serves to capitalize on weaknesses.
Changes grips on volleys.	Has trouble hitting low volleys.	Hit low balls and balls at the body.
"Windshield wiper" grip on volleys (hits all volleys with the same side of the racket).	Has trouble hitting low volleys.	Hit low balls to the volleyer's feet.

Reactions
and Reflexes

You're standing on the baseline waiting to return a serve. Your opponent is an average server on the men's tour and hits his first serve about 120 miles per hour. It takes about one-third of a second for the ball to travel the 60 feet from his baseline and bounce on your service line. After the bounce the ball slows to only half the speed (60 miles per hour). It travels the final 18 feet from the service line to the baseline on your side of the net in just over two-tenths of a second. The elapsed time is about half a second.

At recreational levels with a 60-mile-per-hour serve, the elapsed time from racket to racket is barely over a second. Whether you're on the pro tour receiving bullets or just playing neighborhood-league tennis, you just don't have much time—in that instant, you have to recognize where the ball is being hit, judge its speed and spin, and then prepare your racket. And you haven't even decided how and where to hit the ball (see chapter 7). It sounds very challenging because it is.

Then, consider the speed at which you must react when you are at the net trying to return a passing shot. Or, even more difficult, picture both yourself and your opponent at the net and your time is limited to not much more than the blink of an eye. The conclusion? Without good reflexes, tennis can be a struggle.

The good news is that the exercises in this chapter are all designed to speed up your reflexes. Pick the exercises you like and practice them regularly, and you will improve many of the most time-demanding parts of tennis, including returning serve and reacting quickly at the net.

Think about reactions and reflexes and you can't help but think about Grand Slam winner Lleyton Hewitt.

Description

This exercise requires you and a partner to pair up on a soft surface such as grass to protect your rackets. One of you holds a racket parallel to the ground and the other holds his hands above the throat of the racket with palms facing down. The player with the racket drops it without warning, while the other player tries to catch it before it hits the ground. This exercise is unique in that it not only works on quickness and reflexes but also on dynamic flexibility because you need to bend your knees quickly to catch the racket. Perform the racket drop three times and then rotate positions.

Helpful Tips

1. Begin with your knees slightly bent, as in a ready position; then, to catch the racket, try to bend your knees more to lower your hands. This is a desirable movement for tennis. The opposite is a bend at the waist, definitely not a movement you want on a tennis court.

2. Start with your hands close to the racket and closely watch your partner's fingers to respond quickly to the moment the racket is released. Keep in mind that, on a tennis court, how fast you perceive your opponent's movement and your opponent's shots will determine how fast you react.

Variation

You can use a broomstick or dowel instead of a racket. Using a broomstick also means that you can perform this exercise on a tennis court, because you no longer have to worry about scratching your racket if it falls on the court.

Did you know?

The racket drop exercise is designed to improve your perception and therefore reaction. Players must begin the perception reflex early by tracking the ball as soon as possible across the net. The goal is to judge how quickly it's traveling, and in what direction. With this simple exercise, players will gradually read the ball better and more accurately gauge how much time they have to prepare.

Ball Drop

Description

In this exercise, hold a tennis ball in front of you in one hand with your palm facing down. Then drop the ball and quickly bend your knees to catch the ball. Ideally you are trying to lower your body height by bending your knees more quickly than the ball is falling. As in the racket drop exercise, remember to bend at the knees, not at the waist.

Helpful Tip

To benefit from this exercise, you must drop the ball from your hand, not toss it up in the air. To check yourself, have a friend put a hand flat on top of yours. When you drop the ball, if your hand pushes your partner's hand upward, you have not performed the exercise correctly.

Variations

1. Try this exercise with your right hand and then your left. Then, finally, with one ball in each hand, perform the drill with both hands dropping and catching the balls at the same time.

2. A more challenging exercise is to drop the ball, move your hand quickly in a circle *around the ball,* and then catch it before it bounces, still with your palm facing down.

Volley Butt Touch

Description

Here's a cooperative drill that's very simple yet physically quite challenging. Volley back and forth over the net, but touch the butt of your racket to the ground in between each hit. The two main benefits of this exercise are that you will have to widen your base, thus improving your balance, and that your racket head will end up in a more upward position when you succeed in touching the butt of the racket handle to the ground. Be forewarned, however—this exercise is a bit intense and will be extremely challenging for any player under the intermediate level.

Helpful Tips

1. When the butt of the racket touches the court, your knees should be bent and the top of your racket should be pointed up toward the sky.

2. Minimize bending at the waist to best simulate what can happen on a tennis court.

3. Touch the butt of your racket to the court immediately after hitting the volley and then prepare upright for the next shot by the time your partner contacts the ball. In other words, the actions must all happen very quickly.

4. This exercise is much more difficult and physically challenging than it sounds. Only players without knee problems should participate.

Variations

1. Start with both of you standing across the net from each other on your respective service lines. Volley four balls back and forth with the "butt touch" in the singles half court straight ahead, and then play out the point in the same half court without touching the racket to the ground. Play games until one player reaches 7 points.

2. Use the same variation but do it crosscourt. After playing in one direction, play in the other direction.

3. All these variations work as well with four players.

In Your Face

Description

This drill emphasizes one of the more difficult skills to teach players: dealing with volleys coming right at your face. Pair up with another player who feeds balls right in your face with great frequency but little pace. You may even start off by softly tossing the balls underhand to get used to the challenge. This keeps the exercise safe but also helps players develop the necessary reflexes to successfully hit this shot in real play. Then, as skills improve and confidence builds, the feeder can back up and start hitting the balls harder and with greater frequency.

Helpful Tips

1. Some people may become nervous when balls come at them. Therefore, if necessary, slowly toss just one ball at a time to begin. The goal is to help each other become comfortable and confident.

2. Generally, if you are at the net when a ball comes right at your body, the easiest shot to hit is the backhand volley. However, if the ball comes at your face with a higher trajectory, you may find it easier to take a quick step to the side and hit a forehand volley. If you are right-handed, you will step to the left with your left foot, virtually moving your head out of the way and replacing it with the strings of your racket.

Variations

1. Once you get a feel for this exercise, you can replace the feeder with a ball machine, which is definitely an easier way to get a consistent feed. However, when practicing with a ball machine, keep in mind that ideally you shouldn't hit more than 10 balls in a row. Therefore, either rotate after a certain number of hits with another player or turn the machine off at appropriate intervals. This will keep your focus higher and result in better performance.

2. Set up target areas. Remember that good tennis players don't just get the ball back into play; they become proactive and do something with it. Every shot should have a purpose, even when you are under pressure.

Description

This exercise can speed up anticipation as well as volley skills. Have three players turn away from the net with one feeder on the other side of the net across from them, all of them standing halfway between the net and the service line. Assign each volleyer a number from one to three. With each ball, the feeder calls out a number. The player whose number was called then turns and volleys the ball back over the net. Create a game by setting up target areas and scoring points. This drill helps the players develop reaction skills, anticipation, and balance. It will also help them with movement and positioning. Some tennis experts even say that players should learn to volley with their feet, not with their hands.

Helpful Tips

1. Make sure that the target areas you establish allow you to succeed the majority of the time. You don't want to set out a bull's-eye target such as a single cone and expect to strike it with a ball from 30 feet away.

2. Studies of optimum learning of motor sports report that goals should be achievable about 70 percent of the time.

Variations

1. If you prefer, call out the players' names instead of assigning numbers.

2. Have the volleyers start off facing the feeder. However, after each volley, each volleyer turns 360 degrees. You will probably notice that all the players will be motivated to spin as fast as possible to turn back to face the hitter. The hitter should not worry about hitting two balls in a row to the same volleyer because the players will have time to spin as long as they don't stand around looking at the shot they just hit.

Description

Line up four players in a doubles half court (two on each side of the net) with one of you behind the service line and the partner in front of the service line. It will look somewhat like an "I" formation in football. If either the back or front player crosses the service line into the partner's territory, that team loses the point immediately. This drill will promote good communication between partners—the back player calls off the front player who may be backing up too far for a short lob. One of the back players starts the point with a lob feed. After that, anything goes, but the ball is never allowed to touch the ground. Players compete until one team wins 7 points, and then they switch sides and positions.

Helpful Tip

The front player might be running and jumping backward while the back player is moving in. In this case, the back player needs to be decisive and call off the front player if necessary. Good communications in doubles can prevent all possible collisions.

Variation

Perform the game on the diagonal with the players lining up in a diagonal "I" formation, either in the deuce courts or ad courts.

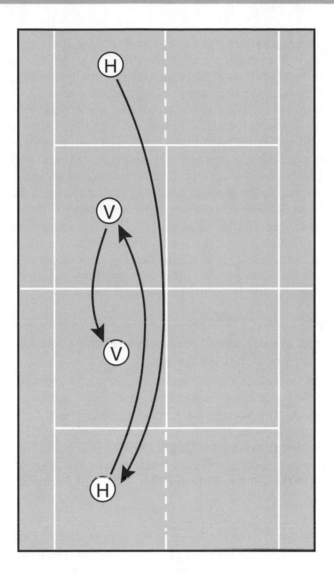

Double Backswing

Description

This exercise is designed to solve the common problem of late preparation on groundstrokes. It is commonly understood that a quick turn begins the backswing for forehands and backhands. But all too often, players find themselves preparing late, therefore hitting the ball late and losing control. To solve this problem, the player about to hit the ball in this drill is required to take two swings at the ball instead of one. This exaggeration exercise works wonders in no time. Prepare the racket as soon as you recognize to which side the ball is coming, take a quick forward swing, and then prepare to hit the incoming ball. After mastering the double swing, try to maintain the early preparation of the double swing but take only one forward swing when it is time to hit the ball. Eventually, you may not prepare that early, but the difference you will feel should definitely help your groundstrokes. Hit 10 balls in a row with a double swing. Then, play 5 regular bounce-hit points from the baseline. Then again, hit 10 balls with the double backswing. Then play 5 double backswing regular bounce-hit points from the baseline. Finally, play 5 regular bounce-hit points from the baseline to finish.

Helpful Tips

1. At first, less experienced players may prefer to toss balls to each other to get accustomed to this exercise.

2. Be sure to "fade" out the double backswing and start to play normally after 5-10 attempts, as explained in earlier portions of this book. By *fading*, I mean that any training aid or guide that will not be present in a real match should be removed at the end of a practice session so that players will not become too dependent on that tool. This prevents you from becoming dependent on certain corrective gimmicks and allows you to make the adjustments and apply them to a normal play situation.

Variations

1. For a challenging exercise, have one player at the net (who will not take a double backswing). This will challenge the player on the baseline even more because he will have less time to perform the exercise.

2. You can use this exercise to practice returning serve.

Description

In this exercise your drill foursome will pair up and start on opposite baselines. Start with one pair of players simultaneously bounce-hitting two balls either crosscourt or down the line at the same time, each ball going to different opponents. Immediately both balls are played out with balls hit anywhere on the court after the initial feed. The winner of each point is determined when the last ball goes out or in the net, and that last ball is the only ball that counts as a point won. The first team to win 11 points wins. Then, switch sides and play again.

Don't let the uniqueness of this drill throw you. Having two balls in play leads to longer practice points, increased focus, faster reflexes and, most of all, fun.

Helpful Tips

1. As far as safety is concerned, while two balls are in play at the same time, the players are not allowed to come to the net and no drop shots are allowed.

2. It is important that both balls be initially hit at approximately the same time.

Variations

1. Two pairs of players exclusively direct their shots crosscourt to the players opposite them. As soon as the first crosscourt pair makes an error and their ball is out of play, they call out loud "miss" and the remaining ball is played out in the full court with all four players involved.

2. Play with the same guidelines, except players can come to the net whenever they want, regardless of whether two balls are still in play or not. You can have fun playing this drill nearly every day for the rest of your career. However, for safety do not perform this variation with hard-hitting, aggressive players.

Doubles Up the Middle

Description

This game is for four players and requires the use of flat or hollow-braided ropes, or even rubber throw-down lines, to create a narrow court. Just lay down the court dividers from baseline to baseline about six feet inside each of the singles sidelines. The four players then play a normal set of doubles within the newly created narrower court. With all angles taken away, play becomes very interesting because players are now hitting exclusively over the lowest portions of the net. The result is a high percentage of shots hit low and down the middle—one of the primary tactics for successful doubles.

Helpful Tips

1. Make sure to use ropes that lie flat on the court for safety. Normal solid-braided round ropes can roll underfoot.
2. Although your reflexes will be tested when you charge the net, there is really no other way to win this game because the possibility of hitting passing shots is completely eliminated.

Variations

1. Move the lines closer together or farther apart, depending on the players' skill levels.
2. You can adjust the placement of the lines to level the playing field in the event that one team is decidedly stronger than the other. Make the size of the court relatively large on the side of the stronger team and smaller on the side of the weaker team.

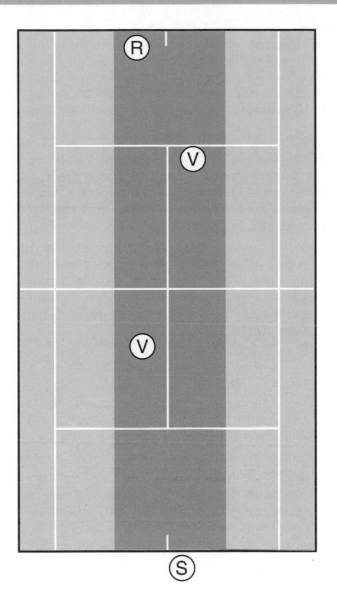

Volley the Serve

Description

This game offers tremendous skill building in both volley reflexes and control and builds confidence at the same time. If you can volley a hard-hit ball such as a serve, normal volleys will be child's play. Pair up with another player; one of you serves while the other stands across the net inside the targeted service box. Play a regular set with both volleys and half volleys allowed on the return of serve.

Helpful Tips

1. This exercise can be intimidating if the server really nails the serves. If you find yourself too nervous about the speed of the incoming serves, have the server slow the serve to half speed to give you the chance to get accustomed to the exercise.

2. Standing on the service line requires the receiver to volley some of the serves and half-volley others. If you find it difficult to make quick decisions whether to hit volleys or half volleys, consider starting by alternating feeding balls to each other from service line to service line. Have the feeder softly tap the serves at first and then build up speed as the receiver improves.

Variations

1. A simplification is to give the receiver points for simply returning the ball over the net and into the court. The other way the receiver can score a point is on missed serves—either in the net or out. The server scores points when the return is missed.

2. You can adjust this game to be easier for the receiver by only allowing the server one serve.

3. To speed up return-of-serve reflexes, have the server hit from the service line and the receiver play from just inside the baseline.

Footwork Skills and Conditioning

To understand the importance of footwork in tennis, just remember *position then preparation*. This catchphrase sums up the fact that being in good position to hit a tennis ball should be higher on your list of priorities than preparing the racket to hit the ball. You can have the best racket preparation in the world, but with the wrong position you will lose many matches 6-0, 6-0. For example, you can prepare thoroughly for a presentation. Your research is immaculate and your notes, slides, and drawings are in perfect order. You dress meticulously and get to the airport early . . . but when the plane lands, you realize you flew to the wrong city. Great preparation but horrible positioning.

Good positioning requires good physical condition, including strength and speed. Plyometric workouts are rapidly becoming an important part of tennis training routines throughout the world. These explosive moves, sometimes against resistance, develop fast-twitch muscle fiber (also known as reflex strength) as well as increased overall strength.

The quick change in exercises in plyometric routines enhances players' ability to find their center of gravity. Players become more conscious of bending their knees, ultimately improving their balance. They develop increased power through a variety of muscles working together at one time in an explosive move. The result is that players get into position earlier and are able to hit the ball more efficiently, with more force and less effort. The movement-based games and drills in this chapter are designed to improve your on-court positioning in a game environment and provide fun experiences at the same time. Isn't that the name of the game?

Many tennis coaches say you should volley with your feet. That means being in the right position is the highest priority at the net.

Description

Here is a simple yet dynamic groundstroke exercise that will challenge you to move better on the court. You will need a partner, coach, or ball machine to feed balls, or you can simply use a backboard. Start on the baseline; when the ball comes to your forehand, move around and hit a backhand. When it comes to your backhand, run around and hit a forehand. This exercise forces you to do a ton of footwork and exemplifies the motto, "Speak less, communicate more." Hit as many consecutive shots as you can comfortably handle, then take a 20- to 30-second break before resuming. Perform the exercise five times with breaks in between.

Helpful Tip

This exercise is even more intense than it sounds. Pace yourself not by lowering your intensity and explosive movement but by hitting fewer consecutive balls. Try hitting just six balls in a row to start, before either rotating with your partner or taking a break. In an average point in tennis, you will seldom hit more than six groundstrokes anyway.

Variations

1. Rally baseline to baseline with a practice partner. After the initial feed down the middle of the court, both of you have to hit two groundstrokes each with your opposite strokes. After that, compete normally.

2. Play a regular set, including a serve, with the following rules: Only one serve is allowed and all shots must be hit with the opposite groundstrokes. Servers begin each game at love-30 because they are at an obvious advantage.

Did you know?

Tennis is essentially an anaerobic sport. Studies have shown that people automatically gain aerobic benefits of workouts when they perform anaerobic exercise. The anaerobic features of tennis are also powerful: An average three-set tennis match requires between 300 and 500 energy bursts.

One-Minute Drill

Description

This drill requires three players. Two are at the net as volleyers on one side of the court with a small basket of balls between them. The third on the opposite baseline is the player performing the drill. The volleyers feed the first ball and keep one point after another going without giving the baseliner a moment to rest. The baseliner tries to win as many points as possible in 60 seconds (timed by one of the volleyers) and receives 2 points for each point won. The baseliner is not allowed to lob, but she can hit into the entire doubles court. The baseliner can reject any feed deemed too difficult and receives 1 point for those bad feeds. Use an honor system, giving the baseliner the last word on which feeds are to be rejected. Keep track of how many points each baseliner wins as each of you rotates around all positions of this high-movement drill.

Helpful Tips

1. The only rule modification to consider is as follows: If you find that the volleyers get too close to the net, lay down a flat rope or some other markers six to eight feet from the net, which they cannot cross.

2. Avoid stepping on or tripping over a ball while running. Clear any loose balls on the court immediately, even if it means stopping the drill and starting again.

Variations

1. Play the same game, but allow lobs.
2. Play for 30 seconds instead of 60.

Double Ready Hop

Description

This exercise is as much a corrective gimmick as it is a movement drill for any on-court situation. A common problem players face is that they simply do not move quickly enough. Generally the result of slow or late movement is poor position and execution. All movements also require a balanced starting action known as the split step or ready hop.

For this exercise, you and your practice partner play minitennis from service line to service line; but instead of taking one split step just before or as your partner hits the ball, squeeze in two. This exercise will get even the most gravitationally challenged players up on their toes and moving. It provides a good workout, and when players shift back to a single split step, they feel as if they have all the time in the world. Hit 10 in a row with double split steps and then 10 in a row with a single split step.

Helpful Tips

1. The trick with this exercise is to complete both split steps *before* or *as* your opponent makes contact with the ball. The split step enables you to get in motion and on balance to help you move in either direction.

2. Remember the law of inertia: A stationary object tends to remain stationary, and a moving object tends to stay in motion. This law of physics is a reminder that the split step is essential in tennis. Without the split step, inertia takes over and you will not be able to move as well as you need to.

3. Remember that after performing the double split step, you need to spend some time taking the normal single split step.

Variations

The variations for this concept in both singles and doubles are endless. Here are a few examples:

1. Play a set of singles and alternate single and double split steps from game to game.

2. Try double split steps only on the return of serve.

3. Volley back and forth with your practice partner (this is an especially tough one).

Counting Steps

Description

This movement and positioning drill is a real winner. Pair up with your practice partner and, before each hit, try to fit in up to eight positioning steps. Remember to count out loud to create more focus. The result will be a significantly increased level of intensity. Start off rallying back and forth cooperatively. Then, once you get a feel for the exercise, play competitively with groundstroke games. Drop shots are not allowed, and play starts with the winner of the previous point bounce-hitting from the middle of the baseline. Play games until one player reaches 11 points.

Helpful Tip

Eight steps are selected as a general rule. Select the number of steps you need to take from table 10.1. The average number of steps taken between shots usually correlates to a player's level of play.

Variations

1. Play this game crosscourt in both directions within the singles half court.
2. Play a regular set with the same rules to most effectively transfer this skill and movement habit to real match play.

Table 10.1	
Ability level	**Number of steps**
Advanced beginners	3–5 steps
Recreational league players	5–8 steps
Advanced intermediate players	8–10 steps
Top competitive players	10–12 steps

Description

This exercise establishes the correct footwork and racket preparation for the volley. You'll need a practice partner who is called your "sparring partner" in this exercise. Have your sparring partner hold two balls, one in each hand, behind his back. The sparring partner's job is to reach out with one of those balls and to take a crossover step as if hitting a volley. As the player with the racket, you face and mirror your partner's movement and present your racket face to the ball that your partner is holding out for you.

At first, alternate slowly from side to side with the proper crossover footwork to get a feel for the exercise. Then, after you establish the proper technique, the sparring partner can randomly make you move to either side as quickly as desired. Don't be fooled: This exercise is for very advanced players as well as beginners. Even highly competitive players can benefit greatly. Try it in 45-second increments and you'll see how challenging it can be.

Helpful Tip

Make sure the volleyer presents the racket to the ball as if to hit it, but she should only lightly brush up against it. Plus, if you are the sparring partner, make sure the volleyer is a friend you can trust.

Variation

Work cooperatively with your sparring partner to see how many times you can lightly touch the ball in that 45-second period.

Groundstroke Side Switch

Description

Here is a baseline movement drill for four players covering the singles court. Points begin with a bounce hit. The two players on each team switch sides with each other every time one of them hits a groundstroke. The result is a huge amount of strategic movement and teamwork. Play until one team reaches 11 points, and then switch sides and play again. Drop shots (defined as any ball that bounces two times within the service boxes) are not allowed.

Helpful Tips

1. The idea is to make players move after they hit. This gets players out of the habit of pausing to watch or admire the shot they just hit.

2. Avoid running into one another when switching sides. If you have any close calls, consider assigning either yourself or your partner to move behind the other player on each switch.

Variation

At lower levels this exercise works equally well with minitennis in the service boxes.

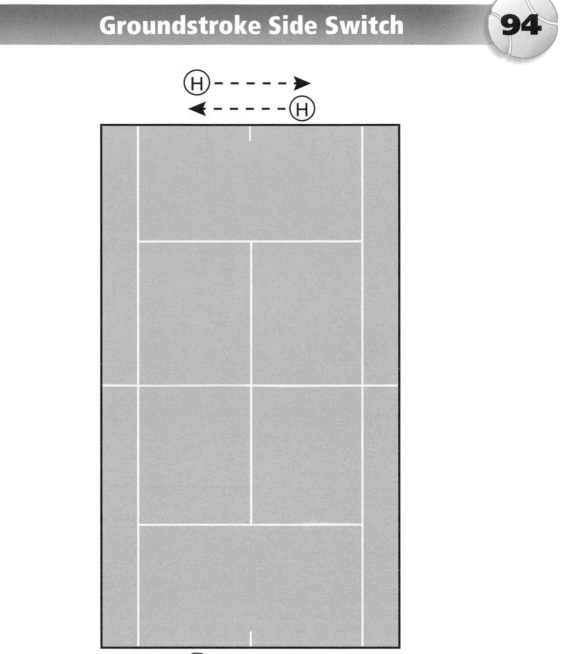

Singles Strategy

Tennis is unique in so many ways. It is one of the few movement sports (with the exception of golf and shuffleboard, which don't require a lot of running) that you can play for your entire life. And what other movement-based sports have competitive opportunities for individuals as well as teams? Basketball, football, baseball, and soccer do not have organized opportunities for one-on-one competition, nor are they sports you can play for a lifetime.

This chapter is a compilation of game-based drills for singles strategy. Almost every drill is adaptable for all levels; only a few are specifically for more advanced players and are noted as such in the descriptions.

All of the games have one thing in common: The rules guide focus and therefore behavior. The rules reward good behavior while discouraging actions that do not follow the rules of the game. I like to call this process *automatic learning* because the players actually learn while having fun and, more often than not, without giving the learning process much thought. It just happens automatically!

Ilie Nastase was one of the best players in the world in his time. His strength, besides being a great tactician, was a talent for creative shot execution.

Description

Ever wonder how to become a more aggressive player? Play a set of singles with your partner; however, after the serve, if you step behind the baseline or outside the singles sidelines, you immediately lose the point. This simple rule adjustment forces a great deal of additional movement and anticipation because more balls will be taken aggressively and on the rise; second, it encourages you to hit the ball with more angles, so your opponent will hit on the run, which is a basic winning strategy in tennis.

Helpful Tip

If you find yourself as the player hitting on the run, realize that you can still be balanced while running. Experts call it *dynamic balance,* which means that you can be on balance while running and hitting a tennis ball as long as you land on balance after contacting the ball.

Variations

1. You may want to limit the lobs to one per point for each player, or perhaps just two lobs per game.
2. Perform the same game but restrict play to the diagonal. You can play crosscourt in the deuce court or crosscourt in the ad court as well.

True Story

In the late 1970s I was part of a team that traveled from island to island in the South Pacific and Micronesia and conducted tennis clinics and played exhibition matches. One of the islands we visited was Truk, a tiny spot surrounded by coral reefs and lush lagoons. One tennis court was on the island. It was built exactly to specifications—so exact that as soon as your foot left the asphalt surface of the playing area, it fell four inches to a surrounding area of grass, dirt, and rocks. The court builders forgot to allow for running room outside the lines. Think of staying within the boundaries of that court surface on the island of Truk when you try playing Inside Singles.

Flow Charting

Description

This idea is more of a technique than a game, but because it covers the all-important competitive issue of momentum, it belongs in this chapter on strategy. Use graph paper to chart your own practice matches. Identify a starting point in the middle of the paper and simply draw a dot up or down on the graph to signify whether a point was won or lost. With each point you win, the dot goes up one square; with each point you lose, the next dot along the line goes down. Then, after you play a set, connect the dots to see the upward and downward momentum of your performance. This is a very simple yet effective way to visualize the importance of momentum. You can also mark off where each game of the set is contained within the chart and whether you won or lost the game.

Helpful Tip

When analyzing your charts, pay particular attention to the first 2 points of each game and, if you won both of those points or lost them, how it affected the outcome of the games themselves.

Variation

You can use the concept to chart patterns in doubles as well.

Player 1

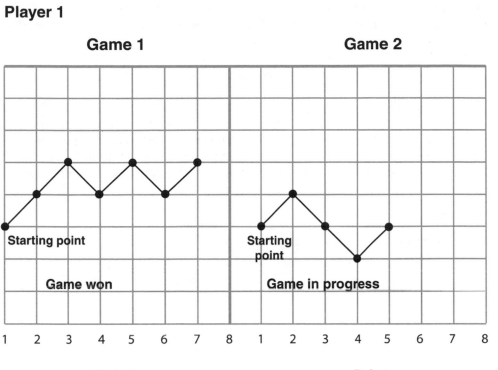

Game 1

Game 2

Starting point

Game won

Starting point

Game in progress

Points

Points

Description

This idea is terrific for social events because it injects lots of fun and laughs into any on-court activity. Just bring some playing cards to the court. Pass out a card for each point won, and play a game of your choice (for example, the first player to reach 100 points wins). In this case, each picture card is worth 10 points and an ace is worth 11. To create even more excitement, show yourselves the card you are competing for.

Helpful Tip

The whole idea of this exercise is to create a fun environment while competing. Try thinking of this drill as fun; and when you are playing a regular match, remember those feelings of enjoyment and try to transfer them to the match situation. In other words, have more fun while competing by remembering fun feelings during your game-based practices.

Variation

This game works well for doubles or singles.

Description

This singles drill encourages you to penetrate deep and straight through the court with your groundstrokes. This is a great tactic against a player who loves to run wide and rip balls crosscourt. You and your practice partner start with a bounce hit. Whichever player hits wide of the sidelines or in the net loses 2 points. However, if you hit the ball long but not wide, you lose only 1 point. Play until one player wins 15 points, and then switch sides.

Helpful Tip

In terms of tactics, the idea of driving through the court has its place in tennis. However, keep in mind that a much higher percentage of groundstrokes in singles should be hit crosscourt rather than down the line.

Variation

If you want to focus on groundstrokes without attacking the net, add the rule that you can go to the net only on short balls, and allow no drop shots. Define a drop shot as any ball that would bounce twice before crossing the service line.

Attached to a Cart

Description

If you ever have access to a teaching cart, you may want to try this singles drill. Play two games holding onto a teaching cart, and then switch roles with your practice partner. This exercise definitely makes the player without the cart aware of the importance of making the opponent move.

Helpful Tip

This exercise may seem to be for fun only, but in fact it forces players to hit high-percentage, well-placed shots, the central strategy of tennis at all levels of play.

Variations

1. With two carts, you could have each singles player hold a cart at the same time.
2. For doubles, use two carts (one on each side of the net), with both players on each team holding either side of the cart.
3. You can also have only one player on each doubles team holding the cart.
4. This is a fun exercise that would work well even for a social tournament.

Description

Here is a two-player deep groundstroke drill with a nice rule variation. To set up the court for this drill, you need to create a horizontal line between the baseline and the service line of the full singles court on both sides of the net. Use either a rope or rubber throw-down lines. You and your hitting partner keep score with continuous out-loud counting. One point is scored for each ball that lands in the deep target area (between the rope and the baseline). If the ball lands in the net, short, long, or wide, there is no penalty; however, winning a point on a deep shot scores double. Play until one player accumulates 50 points. Then, if you want to level the playing field for a rematch, you can handicap the better player by making his deep target area smaller.

Helpful Tips

1. Use flat or hollow-braided ropes that will not roll underfoot.
2. Start with a bounce hit from the baseline and alternate which player begins each point.

Variations

1. Play this game in the down-the-line singles half court.
2. Play in the crosscourt diagonal singles half court in one direction and then the other.
3. Play with two players on each side of the net alternating shots.
4. Four people can play "winner stays" with two players at a time playing out a point while their partners coach them from the side. The on-court player who wins the point stays to play the next point, up to 3 in a row, before rotating with the partner. The player who loses the point, on the other hand, switches positions with her partner immediately.

Did you know?

There are two primary ways to hit the ball deeper in the court. The first is to simply hit it harder. The second is to hit it higher over the net (increasing the arc). Experiment with both and see which one is more effective for you.

Description

In this game-based singles drill, emergency situations are the strategic focus. Either you or your practice partner will assume a baseline position as the feeder while the other player will start off touching the net on the other side of the court. The feeder hits a lob to start the point. The ball must bounce, and it should challenge the receiver enough to force him to hit an emergency wrist-flick shot (see the following detailed description). After that, anything goes, and the point is played out. Rotate every five feeds and continue until one player reaches 21 points.

Helpful Tip

There are three main types of flicks:

1. You run facing away from the net and use your wrist to flick your racket to one side of your body or the other.

2. A high lob goes over your head and you flick your wrist over your head to hit the ball while still running toward your own back fence.

3. We've all seen the pros try the low-percentage shot at one time or the other: Run straight back to the fence and flick the ball between your legs (not recommended for safety reasons).

Variations

1. Play the same game with four on a court.

2. With only two players you can play this game crosscourt in each direction.

3. A slightly more advanced variation is for the emergency shot hitter to call out, "Down the line," or "Crosscourt" before contacting the ball. The point only starts when the flick lands in the correct half of the court.

Strategy

The emergency wrist flick is an extreme shot hit only in extreme situations. You are out of position and on the run. You have no option but to try something radical. So far, so good. The problem is that these flick shots are hardly ever practiced; therefore, in a game they become desperation shots rather than a shot you have a good chance of executing. Because tennis is a game in which emergency situations arise, you must practice these types of shots. Think of it the same way as practicing fire drills, except you can count on being in at least one type of emergency every time you walk on a court to play. It happens to the best of us.

Description

Here's a drill in which you focus on hitting controlled, angled passing shots. You and a partner start with one of you at the net and the other on the opposite baseline. The volleyer starts each point with a bounce hit but, as in many other drills in this book, the baseliner may reject this initial feed if it is too difficult. Lobs are not allowed, and down-the-line passing shots must land in the singles court. However, passing shots hit crosscourt are allowed to land in the doubles alleys. This single rule adjustment encourages a dramatic number of angled passing shot attempts to make this drill not only fun but a real skill builder as well. Rotate positions every 5 points and play until one player wins 15 points. Then, switch sides and play again.

Helpful Tip

This exercise is an example of what I like to call *helpful exaggeration.* Exaggerating the size of the preferred target area (in this case angled crosscourt passing shots) and rewarding the successful attempt with bonus points encourage desired behavior and skill development at the same time. Another point is that the use of helpful exaggeration tools such as expanded target zones should be followed by regular play. As mentioned in chapter 9, this principle is called *fading*—removing any training aid or guide that will not be present in a real match at the end of a practice session so that players will not become too dependent on that tool. You want to maintain the skill that was developed, but the feel for the court at the end of the practice session should be based on reality.

Variations

1. If you want to work on your short crosscourt angles, count only the crosscourt balls that land in the alleys if they bounce short of the service lines.

2. Finally, award 2 points for those balls landing in the alleys if you want to emphasize the crosscourt passing shots.

Description

Statistical analysis of tennis matches started off years ago with the coach sitting at courtside taking notes with pad and pencil in hand. With the arrival of the computer age, the pad-and-pencil technique for charting has generally been forgotten. The idea for this exercise is so simple that players at any level can immediately begin charting and learning more about their own games, both during practice sessions and in real matches. Just choose one specific issue that you want to track and focus on, such as groundstrokes hit into the net. Every time one of these errors occurs, take a ball from a bucket or hopper that you have brought to the court and squeeze the ball into the back fence. Then, at the end of your practice set, make note of how many balls are in the fence to track your focus issue (in this case forehands and backhands hit into the net). All that's needed are some extra balls and a fence. *Simplicity charting* is charting in its most simple form with no need for coach or computer.

Helpful Tips

1. If you are playing indoors and don't have a fence, just place the balls on a bench or in one corner of the court.

2. The simple act of taking a ball and placing it somewhere else draws your focus toward that specific issue. And, simply by concentrating on it, you are bound to improve.

3. Simplicity charting is also a good way to track improvement from week to week. Just keep lists of the totals charted on specific aspects of your game and check your progress over time.

4. Keep in mind that you do not have to chart only mistakes. Charting positive things can be even more powerful. Consider charting the number of points you win at the net or points you win when your opponent comes to the net and that you must counterpunch.

Variations

1. Additional focus issues are virtually unlimited. Just limit it to one issue at a time or, at the most, two things that you can easily monitor.

2. If you are practicing with a friend, you may want to add some extra fun, such as letting your friend choose the focus issue for you.

Doubles Strategy

As the introduction to chapter 11 relates, tennis is one of the few movement sports that you can play for your entire life. Tennis also allows for both individual and team competition. Although doubles tennis is relegated to about 5 percent of the TV coverage (and often only to fill a time slot during rain delays), it plays a much more prominent role in all other levels of the sport. In high school, college, and recreational tennis, doubles is on nearly equal footing with singles and sometimes receives even more emphasis. The most prominent example is the Atlanta Lawn Tennis Association (ALTA), which boasts more than 60,000 citywide participants, the majority of whom play doubles.

In the United States there are about 14,400 high school tennis teams and nearly 1,500 college teams. Success in doubles competition is an essential part of any team's overall success. In fact, doubles is becoming so competitive at collegiate levels that college coaches often interview prospective team members to determine their abilities in doubles, not just their singles records.

This chapter features drills and games to help you play better doubles. If a complete book of singles were written and placed alongside the complete book of doubles, the singles book would be as skinny as Stan

Laurel and the doubles book as large as Oliver Hardy. Most drills are adaptable for all levels, and only a few are specifically for more advanced players and are noted as such in the descriptions. Again, all of the games have one thing in common: They use unique rules to guide focus and therefore behavior. As mentioned in chapter 11, this process is called *automatic learning* because the players actually learn while having fun. It just happens automatically!

Note that chapter 11 contains several games that can be adapted easily to doubles play and are listed in the descriptions as suitable for doubles. In case you jumped ahead to this chapter in search of helpful doubles exercises, you may want to backtrack to the previous chapter.

More recreational league players in the U.S. play doubles than singles. The reason is simple: less court to cover but mentally interesting at the same time.

Description

This is a simple crosscourt serve-and-volley game for two players using the doubles half court. However, because the server has such a huge advantage, he starts the game at 0 and the receiver starts with 7. The first player to reach 11 points wins. This is another excellent exercise for improving doubles skills just through game-situation drilling.

Helpful Tip

Play these games seriously, because players who play tough in drills are undoubtedly tough in real match play.

Variation

To play this same doubles game-situation exercise with four players on the court at the same time, two pairs compete crosscourt and just alternate play. For safety, two balls should not be in play at the same time. You'll find that you have no down time at all because while one team is recovering for the next point, the other pair will be playing.

Lob Volley

Description

If you want to throw anyone into deep water, this exercise will quickly do the trick. Start out on the two service lines with two players on each side of the net. Although fairly simple, this drill is still very effective and has become somewhat of a classic. Hit two volleys back and forth and then a lob volley. After that, the point is played out. If your adrenaline doesn't start pumping with this one, go immediately to your doctor for a check-up!

Helpful Tips

1. If necessary, all four players should warm up their lob volleys before trying this exercise.
2. For safety reasons, if you or your partner hit a short lob volley and one of your opponents is about to hit an overhead, remember to turn your back if you are still standing around the service line. From that close a distance, don't trust your reflexes to get you out of trouble. Better safe than sorry. The nice thing about tennis is that losing one point seldom makes the difference between winning and losing.

Variations

1. To adjust this exercise for two players, just have them play in the singles half court straight ahead for a fun and exciting variation.
2. Have two players play this same exercise but only crosscourt either in the deuce court or in the ad court to ensure that the players are working on the execution of all possible shots and angles.

Five Balls

Description

This game-based drill is as much fun as it is fast-paced. Start out with two sets of five balls on the ground, one set against the net on each side of the court. Two teams start on opposite baselines, and a spin of the racket decides which team will start by running to the net and feeding the first ball into play. Subsequently, the team who wins the point feeds the next ball. The first team to feed all of the balls on their side of the net as well as win the final point when they have no balls remaining wins the game. Obviously, the only additional rule is to allow the receiving team to reject the feed. This forces the feeding team to hit a returnable feed on the first shot. The team that uses up all five balls on their side of the net wins the drill. This game is designed to get all four players on their toes.

Helpful Tips

1. Although the rules of this drill allow players to reject the feeds that are not returnable, don't think that this forces you to hit super-easy shots with the first ball. Drop shots, sharp angles, and lobs can all put your opponents on the move and off balance, exactly what you want in a real match situation.

2. The team that receives the feed can move wherever they want in the court. They can stay back on the baseline, move to mid-court, or rush the net.

Variations

1. If you want to create even more movement, add the rule that both players of the receiving team must touch the net with their rackets before returning the feed.

2. Create additional movement by having the receiving team touch the back fence with their rackets before moving into the court to return the feed.

Description

This exercise is a dynamic, competitive doubles drill to get teams to close in to the net and attack as quickly as possible. It also encourages servers to increase the spin on their serves and encourages receivers to move in quickly to take the returns as early as possible. The main rule is that the serve is the only shot that is allowed to bounce! This adjustment forces an increased attacking style that can help all levels improve. It also encourages the server's partner to be more active at the net. The only additional rule is that no lobs are allowed.

Helpful Tips

1. Serving more slowly by hitting spin serves gives the server more time to run closer to the net.

2. Although the tendency will be to charge into the net, remember to be on balance as far as possible before hitting your first volley.

3. This exercise should perk up the server's partner to a higher energy level than ever before. Just remember to transfer that same high level of movement and alertness to real match play.

Variations

1. For the most competitive levels, allow lobs, but not on the return of serve.

2. "Two-Bounce Doubles" is a variation that allows both the serve and the service return to bounce. After that, all balls must be hit out of the air.

3. For less advanced players, allow one bounce on each side in addition to the serve during each point.

Description

This is a game-based drill to get players of all levels to come to the net. Start with all four players on the baseline in a groundstroke rally with no drop shots allowed. A fifth player or onlooker is assigned the task of calling out, "Go!" to signal all four players to immediately charge the net. If an error is made before "go" is called, the rally must start again, but no points are scored. Play games until one team wins 11 points, and then change sides or rotate partners. It's simple, it works, and it's fun.

Helpful Tips

1. This game adapts easily for singles.
2. This is also a great drill if you are part of a team workout with many players on several courts at a time.

Variations

1. Beginners can perform the same exercise starting on the service lines playing minitennis.
2. Start with a bounce hit with all four players on the baseline, but this time you must all cooperate by hitting four shots in a row before the point is played out. On the fourth hit, all four players may charge the net. Award 2 bonus points if both team members are in front of the service line when they win the point.
3. Assign one of the four players to call out "go" for 3 points in a row, after which the responsibility rotates to another player. However, the assigned player also has another task: As soon as that person calls "go" she has to run and touch the back fence before moving toward the net. This rule really gets the partner of the player who calls "go" to hustle to help cover their team's side of the court.

Minidrop

Description

All four players play out a variation of the standard game of minitennis doubles in the service boxes, starting points with a bounce hit. The unique feature of this game is that the team that wins the point immediately drops the next ball off the edge of the net. The only other rules are that all balls must be hit with backspin (underspin) and no smashes are allowed. Each ball must bounce once on each side of the net. The first team to win 7 points wins; then switch sides. You will find that this exercise is similar to some of the ball-control drills in chapter 1, except that the drop off the edge of the net creates an additional element of unpredictability and excitement.

Helpful Tips

1. The drop off the net brings the players in very tight to the net at first. A common mistake is to then stay there. Players must immediately back off toward the service line because all balls must be allowed to bounce. If players don't back off quickly, they will be immediately out of position and in big trouble.

2. Remember that minitennis means no hard hitting. If anyone hits a shot too hard, you can call out "replay." Just make sure to call it out before hitting the shot. It is not appropriate to go for a ball, miss it, and then decide that the incoming ball was hit with too much power. Minitennis play focuses on direction, spin, and control.

Variations

1. Play the same game, but the two players on each side of the net must alternate shots within each point.

2. To add more movement, have the players alternate shots as explained previously, except each player has to run and touch the baseline after each shot.

3. A natural extension is to play the same game, but after the drop, play is allowed on the entire court with no restrictions.

Strategy

Although a drop shot or sharply angled ball is appropriate in doubles, generally it is not advised. The reason is that if the drop shot does not win the point (which it seldom does), it is most likely an invitation to your opponents to come to the net. And, in doubles, the net is the one place you prefer your opponents not to be.

Inside Doubles

Description

The rules of this game automatically speed up play for recreational doubles. At the same time, it will speed up your reflexes and reactions through the use of only one special rule: After the serve, all four players must stand inside the doubles sidelines for all their shots. Stepping behind the baseline or outside the doubles sidelines leads to an immediate loss of point. Play normal sets. This exercise forces a great deal of additional movement and anticipation, plus more balls will be taken aggressively on the rise. Note that drill 97 (page 148) contains a similar exercise for singles.

Helpful Tip

Policing these rules can be challenging at times because a player can quickly step outside the lines with one foot and immediately bring it back over the line. Sometimes a player may not even be aware that a rule infraction took place. If all players understand that the rules are in place to help everyone improve, it will help.

Variations

1. With this rule in place, you may want to limit each team to one lob per point.

2. You can also allow just one total lob per point for both teams. In other words, as soon as either team hits a lob, no players on either side are allowed to hit another lob for the rest of that point.

Description

This exercise is possible only with the use of an air target set up three to four feet over the net. An air target can consist of a rope or bungee cord tied to telescopic poles that raise the height of the net, or you can simply tie a rope from side fence to side fence if you are playing on an individually fenced court. Play normal doubles with the rule that all balls must pass above the net but under the horizontal line. After trying this, you'll quickly see that the techniques required to keep balls low in doubles develop nearly on their own. Learning experts call this *guided discovery*.

Helpful Tip

An alternative to rope or bungee is a thin ribbon. You can use any material that is visible enough to see from the baseline yet small enough that the ball will not hit it repeatedly.

Variation

If the level of play is too low to consistently hit this low over the net, adjust the rules to allow each team one ball over the line on each point. But the moment the second ball in a single point goes over the raised net line, the point is lost. You also have the option of raising the horizontal line, which is an easy adjustment to make if you are tying the rope from fence to fence or using telescopic poles.

Did you know?

In tennis there are two types of targets: primary and secondary. Primary targets are like windows above the net that your shots pass through. Secondary targets are where balls bounce on the court. Although it is common to practice with secondary targets, which can be as big as service boxes or as large as the area between the service line and baseline, players set up primary targets much less frequently. When setting up any kind of targets, whether they be primary or secondary, be sure to make the target big enough so that you can succeed in striking it (or hitting through it in the case of primary targets above the net) about 70 percent of the time. This level of success should be substantial enough to keep you coming back for more.

Handling Match Pressure

Groundstrokes, volleys, serves and returns, tactics and strategy for singles and doubles, team games, and reflex and movement skills have all been examined and drilled in a game-based environment. And we're confident that you and your practice partners have had hours of fun at the same time. After all, if we have fun while practicing, chances are we will keep at it and improve at the same time. But we have one more door to open: how to handle match pressure.

Thousands of players throughout the world look great and move great on a tennis court. But as soon as they get in a real match they tighten up. Some people compare it to driving a car with the emergency brake on or to gargling with peanut butter (choking!).

Before 1968 (the year the open era began), when competitive tennis was played only on the amateur level, it all seemed so innocent. There were traditions of championships, including all the Grand Slam events, as well as Davis and Fed Cup competitions. But now, because so much money is devoted to professional sports, it seems that everyone wants a piece of the action: agents, sponsors, and (sometimes the most dangerous of all) overeager parents of blossoming superstars. Unfortunately, it is not uncommon for parents of children only seven and eight years old to become starstruck and start charting out their future star's career.

On the positive side, sport psychologists agree that healthy competition can actually do people a world of good. A little friendly tennis competition can build and reinforce self-confidence and self-esteem. It can even help us recognize and confront some of our own personal fears, which some call the monsters in our minds. Fear of failure, fear of lack of recognition, fear of embarrassment, and fear of lack of acceptance based on performance are just a few. But we also need to know that some fears have a good purpose. For example, fear of failure can motivate us to practice harder and increase our focus. Just don't let a fear interfere with your ability to play your best. Turn a fear into motivation and it can ultimately become a friend. The best way to accomplish this is to follow the old tennis adage of "play as you practice and practice as you play."

The games in this chapter are designed with one purpose in mind: to put pressure on you in an enjoyable game situation. After all, if you identify real match pressure with fun, when the day of reckoning arrives, you may actually enjoy it!

Venus Williams has handled match pressure since her debut on the pro tour. She goes for her shots, regardless of the score and situation.

Practice Making Errors

Description

This exercise asks you to do something you seldom do: intentionally make errors to learn how to deal with them. In this drill, you and a practice partner play a tiebreaker. But without warning, in the middle of any point, a third player or coach calls out "miss" or blows a whistle. Then, whoever's turn it is to hit the ball must intentionally make an error. The score changes accordingly and play continues. Both players are now forced to cope with a new mental situation. This drill gets you accustomed to reacting to this inevitable circumstance with renewed focus, rather than becoming distracted.

Helpful Tips

1. The observing player should call out, "Miss" or blow a whistle at least three times in a tiebreaker and, if you're playing a regular set, once or twice per game. "Miss" should be called out as a ball is crossing the net, not too early, and not too late.

2. If a player hears the signal but does not miss the shot, the point is replayed because the issue is to mentally interfere with your concentration and not just to change the score.

Variations

1. This game can be played with doubles as well as singles.
2. If desired, even a nonplaying friend can be the whistle blower and you can play regular sets.

Three-Point Gamble

113

Description

For this game, you and your drilling partner will be guided to seek opportunities to hit winners. Play starts from the baseline with a bounce hit; either player can, at any given time, call out "winner" just before hitting the ball. For every clean winner (that is, one that the opponent cannot even touch), 3 points are awarded. However, if you make an error on your attempt at a winner or the opponent simply touches the ball, you lose 3 points. The obvious benefit is that you will begin to look for opportunities to hit winners, a quality found in successful players. Play games to 21 points to keep the scoring simple.

Helpful Tips

1. Make sure to call out, "Winner" loudly and clearly.
2. Be aware that going for winners is fine as long as you are able to succeed more often than fail in your attempts. In other words, although this drill encourages you to go for winners, making errors comes with a price. In this game, the price is the loss of 3 points.

Variations

1. This drill works just as well for doubles with all four players starting with a bounce hit on the baseline.
2. Give the player 2 points if "winner" is called and the opponent touches the ball but cannot return it. Give him 3 points if the "winner" cannot even be touched. This variation encourages everyone to put in the extra effort to try to return shots that may appear out of reach.
3. Make the gamble worth only 2 points instead of 3, and count winning shots that just win the point, instead of just "clean" winners.
4. For doubles, allow the players to come to the net after four groundstrokes.

Wild Card

Description

This is a competitive game. Play a tiebreaker with your practice partner, and have a third player or coach call out "wild card" or blow a whistle at any time. Then, whether you are just about to start or already in the middle of a point, those wild card points score double if any of you hits a clean winner (one that the opposing player cannot even touch). However, if you go for a winner but lose the point, you only lose 1 point. After each tiebreaker, rotate positions with the other players.

Helpful Tips

1. This game works well for a variety of levels and adapts to many other competitive drills in this book.

2. This game encourages you to experiment and gamble, yet you need to be aware of the consequences if you miss.

Variations

1. Play doubles instead of singles.

2. Make clean winners worth 3 points instead of 2.

3. Redefine "winner" as any point-winning shot rather than a shot that cannot be touched.

4. Start with a bounce hit with both you and your partner starting on opposite baselines.

5. If you have a nonplaying friend who doesn't mind helping while watching you play, play a full set, or better yet, two out of three.

Allowable Unforced Errors

Description

In tennis, the number of "unforced errors" should neither be too many or too few. In other words, players should know that they can afford to miss a certain number of shots, and they should be aware of that number. The goal should be challenging but achievable. Here's a way to increase your awareness of allowable unforced errors on court.

First, you need to set a goal. Try limiting yourself to 10 unforced errors in a set as a starting point. Then, depending on how you play, make adjustments in future sets to sufficiently challenge yourself, but also be realistic. Play a practice set of singles. Each time either you or your practice partner makes an error, mark it down on a piece of paper on the side of the court. This exercise also works easily with players of slightly different abilities. Just assign a different number of allowable unforced errors to each player. Then, no matter who wins the set, if you both stay within your allowable number of unforced errors, you will both have reached the performance goals you have set for yourselves in this drill. Of course, as you progress, gradually reduce the number of allowable errors.

Helpful Tips

Sometimes, defining an unforced error can be challenging or even confusing. For example, is it an unforced or a forced error when your opponent hits a tough first serve and you miss the return? Or, what is it when your opponent hits a moderately effective approach shot and you hit a passing shot attempt wide? These decisions will always be somewhat subjective; however, here are two general guidelines to get you started:

1. If you miss a shot that your tennis skills allow you to successfully hit 70 to 80 percent of the time, consider it an unforced error.
2. Any shot you cannot control into the court hit at that 70- to 80-percent success rate is a forced error.

Variations

1. If you have extra practice balls and are playing on an outdoor court with a fence, just squeeze a ball in the fence, which will represent each of your allowable errors.
2. This concept works equally well for doubles.

Description

As a follow-up to the previous exercise, this game-based drill creates an even more holistic exercise by giving you and your practice partner a chance to "erase" your posted unforced errors. As in the previous drill, play a set and use pencil and paper or squeeze balls into a fence to track your number of allowable unforced errors. The rule adjustment is that any outright winner erases one of the errors. So, if you hit a winner, walk to your tally sheet, pick up your pencil eraser, and cross out one of those errors. Or, if you are keeping track by squeezing extra balls into one area of the fence, walk over and pull out one of those balls.

Helpful Tip

If possible, use the "ball in the fence" method of keeping track. That way there is no possibility of anyone secretly adjusting the tally of unforced errors, and the increased visual aspect of publicly displaying your unforced errors in a fence should help increase your focus as well.

Variations

1. You can keep two groups of balls or two columns on your piece of paper: one to represent unforced errors and one for those that are forced.

2. As with so many of the drills in this book, this one works equally well for doubles.

Strategy

In recent years, professional tennis match commentators have added a new statistic to analyze: the winner-versus-unforced-error ratio. Of course, years ago many top coaches charted this statistic, but it was never publicized so broadly as we see now. Top players in the world try to hit more winners than unforced errors. This may sound simple, but it is actually very difficult. Try tracking your own winners versus unforced errors and you'll find out for yourself.

Distraction Tennis I

Description

One of the biggest challenges in competitive tennis is to keep players focused and to limit the distractions that can wreak havoc on a player's concentration. This exercise is designed to increase your ability to focus even while in the middle of distractions. Rally with your partner down the middle of the court from baseline to baseline while two other players stand in the doubles alleys right next to the net hitting sharp crosscourt angles. Because two balls will be in play at the same time, all four players will have to focus carefully on their own balls. Challenge each pair to hit 20 balls in a row and then switch positions.

Helpful Tip

Players in all positions should play this drill energetically. In other words, even though it is a controlled, cooperative exercise, all four players should be active and on their toes, always taking split steps and moving energetically as if it were a real match.

Variations

1. You can make this game competitive: The pair hitting short crosscourts can aim for the alleys short of the service lines and play out points. On the baseline, just play out points and require that all balls land behind the service lines.

2. With six players, have two short crosscourt rallies going on at the same time.

3. For 10 players, add two pairs hitting crosscourt groundstrokes from the deep baseline corners as well.

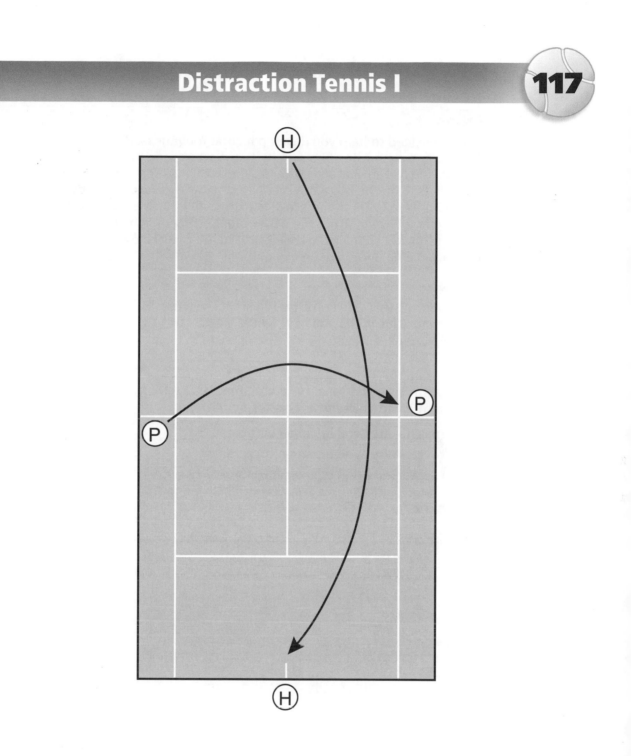

Changing Rackets

Description

Here's a drill designed to help you develop mental toughness. Both you and your drilling friend each bring two rackets to the court, one for playing and one as a backup. Play a normal set; however, whoever misses a first serve has to change rackets to hit the second serve. The situation you are simulating is what you would have to do if you broke a string while hitting a first serve. Typically, players get psyched out when they break strings and have to switch to their second racket. This game-based drill helps players overcome this obstacle by practicing under adverse conditions.

Helpful Tip

Your mind-set during this drill is critical toward its success. Think of yourself in a real match situation when you have just broken a string. It might happen sooner than you think, and you'll be prepared instead of surprised.

Variations

This theme has many variations. Here are some examples of situations in which you can drill with switching rackets:

1. Switch rackets after you hit a ball in the net.
2. Switch rackets after you hit an unforced error.
3. Switch rackets after you miss a return of serve.

Did you know?

Pete Sampras is one of the best players in the history of the game. How many rackets would Pete have ready in case a string broke? Pete travels with his own racket stringer and, whether or not he even takes a single frame out of his bag, all 10 of his rackets get restrung each day he has a match or practice session.

Tug-of-War 119

Description

This game is one of my favorites. It helps develop mental toughness and will force you to focus on winning back-to-back points to gain and maintain momentum. Serve out singles points where the winner of the last point serves the next one. The unique feature of this drill is the scoring. Only one number, called the court score, is kept on the court. Start with the court score at 5. The goal for one of you is to reach 10 and for the other player to reach 0. Simply add or subtract points depending on who wins each point. For example, if you are the player going for 10 points and you win the first point, the court score simply becomes 6. The winner of each point serves the next one, starting in the deuce court.

Helpful Tip

If you use this drill for a team workout, just anticipate that each game can take a long time to play. Like a seesaw, the score tends to keep going up and down.

Variations

1. Handicapping uneven abilities is easy with this drill. Just start the court score with the weaker player closer to his or her goal.
2. Doubles as well as singles can be played.

120 Momentum Drilling

Description

This hitting drill is a terrific exercise for recognizing and fighting to gain the momentum needed for successful tennis. Although there are many ways to play this drill, just cover the singles court with your partner. Points start with a down-the-middle bounce hit from the baseline from the player who won the previous point. Single points won are called minipoints. Three back-to-back minipoints constitute one maxipoint, the goal of the drill. The result of this scoring is a tug-of-war battle with many minipoints but few maxipoints awarded. Play until one player wins 5 maxipoints, and then switch sides to play again.

Helpful Tip

Because the scoring can get repetitious in this game, the player starting each point should call out the score.

Variations

1. This drill works well as a handicap system to level the playing field for two uneven players. For example, a maxipoint for the stronger player can require 4 minipoints in a row, but the weaker player may only need 2.

2. Play this game with four players starting on the baseline with a bounce hit. Whichever player wins the point feeds the next ball into play.

2. Play either singles or doubles, beginning each point with serving. You can elect to allow either one or two serves.

Tennis' Two-Point Play

Description

In this game-based drill, the rules create pressure early in each game to raise your level of concentration. With a practice partner, play a set in which all points when the first serve is missed are worth 2 points. For example, if the server misses the first serve on the first point, winning that single point can then send the server or receiver ahead 30-0 depending on which player wins the point. This rule encourages consistent first serves as well as tough play when you either serve or receive second serves.

Helpful Tips

1. The idea is to encourage the server to get all first serves in during an entire game to avoid 2-point plays, because it would give the receiver an increased chance to break serve.
2. This exercise increases the receiver's awareness that returning second serves in a match is an opportunity to break serve.

Variations

1. Use these rules to play a set of doubles.
2. Instead of awarding 2 points to the winner of points that start with a second serve, give those points a 3-point value.

122 Win Last Point or Back to Love

Description

This game-based exercise is incredibly simple yet highly effective. Play a set of singles with your practice partner, and make a special scoring adjustment to place total emphasis on winning game points. Any player who has a game point yet loses that point returns back to love or 0. Let's say that you are playing a match and you are serving at 40-15. If you win the point, it would be your game; however, if you lose that point your score goes back to love and the new score is now love-30. In this case, on the next point, you would again serve to the deuce court. Another example is if you are the receiver and you have a breakpoint at 30-40. This time, if you don't convert that opportunity, the score changes to 40-0 for the server.

Helpful Tip

The rule adjustment of this game is not only terrific for practices but also for social tournaments.

Variation

This drill works equally well for doubles.

Group and Team Training

This chapter follows the natural sequence from the previous chapters that featured game-based drills for singles and doubles. Here we focus on group tennis, which is more common than you might think. Here are just 10 of the many group situations in tennis:

- High school teams
- College teams
- League teams
- Junior development programs
- All group drill sessions
- Tennis camps for juniors
- Tennis camps for adults
- Tennis birthday parties
- Tennis carnivals
- School physical education classes

The games and drills in this chapter are generally game-based. Some of them do not require a coach; others do require a coach, instructor, or better player to participate with the group. Some games and drills are designed for four on a court, some for six, some for eight, and some for groups larger than that. The one common element is fun and movement. Gone are the days of group instruction when players tolerate standing in a line, waiting to be fed a single ball from their teacher who shouts instructions from across the net. In fact, I surveyed 150 adult recreational players and asked them to list the things they did not enjoy in group tennis classes. The top three things they disliked most were as follows:

1. Standing in lines
2. Shadow swinging
3. Being shouted at from across the net

Keep these issues in mind the next time you are in a group tennis lesson. Suggest that the teacher consider replacing some of the old line drills with some of the game-based drills from this chapter. At the very least, everyone will feel more involved and probably have a lot more fun!

Whether you're playing a senior event at the U.S. Open or a club tournament, you'll play better with proper preparation.

Description

This group game helps players develop the skills required for a drop volley. You'll need at least six players (two teams of three on each side of the net) on your court for this drill. The players cannot let the ball bounce, they cannot hit overheads or power shots, and each player on the team must volley the ball once when the ball is on his side. If necessary, you can also allow one or more bounces per side depending on the level of the players. Play games until one team reaches 15 points and score just as in volleyball.

Helpful Tips

1. The skills needed for passing a ball from one team member to another are almost identical to the skills needed for a drop volley.
2. Each team may want to pair up two players to pass balls back and forth as a practice exercise before starting to compete.

Variations

1. Change the passing rule to two passes per side no matter how many players are on the court.
2. On the other end of the scale, you can extend the control needed by requiring each player on each team to contact the ball twice before passing it over the net.

124 Champs and Challengers

Description

This is a fast-paced game with four players (two on each side of the court) all starting with their rackets on top of the net. One team is the defending champion and the teams across the net are challenging to take over their spot. You can comfortably have up to eight players per court rotating in teams of two to challenge the champs. To start the point, a coach or another player randomly feeds a ball to the challengers. Points are then played out in the entire doubles area. For the challenging team to replace the champs, they have to win 2 points in a row. If the challengers lose the first point, however, they move to the end of the line and the next pair steps forward to take their chances.

Helpful Tips

1. The feeder can adjust the feeds to keep the score as close as desired.
2. This game is guaranteed to speed up player recovery patterns and reflexes because each point starts at full speed and is unpredictable.

Variations

This concept can be used with many rule variations. Here are a few to get you started:

1. Champs start on the service line. Challengers start on the baseline and are fed a short ball.
2. Champs start at the net; challengers start on the baseline. Champs are fed a lob to hit an overhead to start each point.
3. Champs start on the baseline and are fed a high, short sitter. Challengers start on the baseline.
4. Champs start at the net and are fed a volley. Challengers start on the baseline.

Description

In this doubles game your foursome plays a regular set with one important adjustment: Your whole group must continuously run to play the next point as soon as each point is finished. The server must always have two balls ready before serving the next point with the incentive to serve even if the opponents are not in position to return. Point after point, play is fast and exciting. Still switch sides on odd games and everyone will end up sprinting to the other side to quickly resume play. After about 10 minutes a full set should be completed, and you will all have gained quite a workout. The idea is that every point is reactionary and forces you to use just your instincts.

Helpful Tips

1. In the case of uneven matchups, tell the better player or team that only one serve is allowed.

2. Remember to break for water after every five minutes if the weather is very hot.

Variation

Because this is a chapter on group and team games, consider this exercise the next time you are out with a league team or large group. Play this game and, after each 10-minute set, have the winning teams rotate up a court in one direction and the losing teams move in the other. Of course, with court rotations, all courts must finish their matches at approximately the same time. Therefore, instead of regular sets, play a total of nine games or any other fixed number. In the case of nine total games, the final score could be 9-0, 8-1, 7-2, 6-3, or 5-4.

Description

The rules are extremely simple in this game-based drill. Play doubles, and the first team to reach four games wins the set. This rule increases emphasis on getting off to a good start in each set. This is also a good rule modification for a social tournament when the organizers want the players to play with as many different players as possible.

Helpful Tips

1. If you find yourself in a tournament with modified rules to shorten play, remember that conditioning will play less and less of a role in the outcome. Therefore, make sure not to pace yourself; rather, put more energy into every point.

2. When playing matches, you also have to consider the effect of temperature and weather conditions on play. For example, if you are in a very humid climate with intense sun, make sure to pace yourself; protect yourself with a hat, sunglasses, and sunscreen; and drink plenty of water. However, if the weather is cool and you are playing at night, weather conditions are of little concern. Although these issues seem obvious, you would be surprised at how many players ignore these considerations and suffer the consequences.

Variation

You can adjust the length of each match in many ways. Just consider the time that you have to play and the number of players and courts.

Description

This exercise builds many tennis-specific skills and encourages teamwork in an atmosphere of fun. Divide up the group so that four players are playing doubles on each court, except one team must play with rackets and the other team must catch and throw. The only guideline for the throwers is that they must throw the ball within three seconds and can only take one step. You may be surprised that the players without their rackets are often as effective as those with rackets.

Helpful Tips

1. For beginning players who may have trouble catching the ball, simply have them block it with their hands and pick up the ball from the court before throwing it over the net.

2. When playing this game, you will observe many tennis-specific skills: movement and positioning, ball placement and tactics, catching ability that resembles controlled volley skills, and communication and team-work for doubles.

Variations

1. Have one player on each team play with a racket and one without.

2. Play a set with no rackets; all players just catch and throw.

3. You can adjust this game to even larger groups, such as junior development programs, with eight players or more on each side of the net. In that case, toss the ball underhanded and don't let it bounce on either side of the net. If you want to create even more fun, play with two balls at a time, and whichever team lets either ball bounce on its side first loses the point.

Description

This drill closely resembles the childhood ball game many of us grew up with. It works well with an even number of players, either four or six, divided up evenly on the court. With four players, one is on the baseline and one is at the net on each side of the court. With six, two play from the baseline, and still only one is at the net. Play starts with a bounce hit from the baseline. The backcourt players use rackets to hit what most resembles passing shots, and the players at the net try to intercept the passing shot attempts by catching the balls with their bare hands. Use volleyball scoring and play games until one side reaches 11 points.

Helpful Tips

1. At beginning or intermediate levels lobs can be allowed.
2. For players having trouble catching the ball, encourage them to block it with both hands and catch it after one bounce to win the point.

Variation

With an odd number of players, place a single player in the middle monkey position to catch any ball possible. After a successful catch, that player switches positions with the player who hit that ball. With three or five players, just rotate around and play for 10 minutes. Whether or not you keep score, this game is loads of fun.

Description

About 20 years ago, no-ad scoring was successfully introduced to competitive tennis in many circumstances to shorten match playing time. This scoring limited the number of points per game to 7, thus increasing player focus on 3-all points. We'll take this concept one step further in this game-based exercise. The first person to win 2 points in any game wins that game. If the score goes to 1-all, the game is decided by 1 no-ad point with the receiver choosing the service box the server will serve into.

Helpful Tip

When you drill with rules meant to increase intensity to get you accustomed to playing under pressure, pretend you are in a real match. Then, when you actually get in a real match pressure situation, you won't be surprised by the feelings of pressure. Soldiers go through combat training for this very reason—to prepare them for battle so that in the face of real fighting they don't go into shock.

Variations

1. A variation is to play 5-point focus games with the no-ad point played at 2 points each.
2. You can also simply play 1-point games. It doesn't get shorter than this!

True Story

If you have ever played a tiebreaker and found yourself quickly down 3-0, you know that losing can happen faster than you would sometimes expect. The purpose of the "Focus Games to 3 and 5" drill and the variations is to increase player focus. It's easy to say that some points are more important than others, but the idea is to play equally well all the time. The legendary Jimmy Connors comes to mind. You can hardly imagine him having a lapse in intensity and concentration. In fact, once on the seniors tour, he was playing David Lloyd and was down several match points. Connors came through and won the match but was asked in the interview afterward if he had been nervous because he had never before lost to David Lloyd. Connors replied, "Nervous? Why should I be nervous? The ball doesn't know what score it is, and I play the same all the time."

Kamikaze

Description

This group drill can comfortably accommodate 8 to 12 players on a single court. Pair up the players into doubles teams and divide them into an even number of teams on each side of the net. On one side of the net, the first team in line serves and volleys Kamikaze style. This means that the server on the serving team closes into the net as quickly as possible to prevent the receiving team's return from bouncing. The receiving team, on the other hand, tries to defeat the serving team and rotate to the other side of the net.

To win and switch sides, however, the receiving teams must accomplish two things: Get the return to bounce on the server's side of the net and win the very same point. All the server's partner at the net must do is touch the ball. It doesn't even have to be hit over the net. This encourages players to find their range at the net because the repercussions of missing are minor. However, each time any serving team loses a point, there is a minor penalty. Each serving team keeps their own score of that lost point and, when the total reaches 3 lost points, the serving team switches sides with whichever receiving team happened to win that third point.

This is a fast-paced drill with a great deal of movement and side switching. Both the serving teams and receiving teams rotate with the other teams on their side of the court after each point is played. Also, the partners of each serving and receiving team alternate positions after each point is played so that everyone keeps on their toes and stays fresh.

Helpful Tips

1. Do not allow lobs on the return of serve.
2. To keep play moving quickly, consider giving the serving team just one serve.
3. Play for a while in the deuce court and then switch to the ad.

Variations

1. If you have dozens of players, you can move teams in a larger circle than just around one court. With four courts of players, for example, instead of switching teams from end to end on each court, rotate the teams in a big circle around all the courts. Just alternate the side of the court teams serve from so that on one side of the bank of courts players alternate from serving to receiving and back to serving again.

2. This kind of game has many possible rule variations. One of my favorites is to start both members of the serving team on the baseline. Again, no lobs are allowed on the returns. This rule forces both players of the serving team to hustle to get in to the net because there will be no chance of poaching on the return.

Love the Battle

Description

Divide as many players as you have in your group into teams of two or up to four, and spin a racket for serve. Have each player on each team play one game against a player from the other team. But a game consists of only one point! A set consists of the first team to win 6 points. However, if the team loses set point, its score goes back to 0. This way each point is a big point and each set point is even bigger! The rules make this game just like 1-point elimination tournaments, but probably more fun because team support is part of the package.

Helpful Tip

Avoid the tendency to go for a big shot when it's your turn at bat. This doesn't mean to play below your normal level; rather, it means to play your normal game. Going for big shots is usually the fast road to making unforced errors.

Variations

1. Allow just one serve.
2. If you have enough players, you can turn this into a doubles tiebreaker by pairing up the players into doubles teams.
3. Play either one-set matches, two out of three, or three out of five, depending on how much time you want to spend on the activity.

For a Change of Pace

Did you ever measure the length of all the lines on a tennis court? There's a total length of 490 feet! Now ask yourself whether you have ever walked onto a tennis court and said to yourself, "Boy, is this an interesting-looking tennis court!" Of course not.

Am I suggesting that you take a can of paint and draw pictures on a tennis court to make it more interesting? No. What I am suggesting is that you can easily create games and drills to change your angle of vision and on-court experience. It will give you a fresh perspective, you will focus more, and you'll have more fun. Although there are hundreds of possibilities of perspective-changing drills, the ones in this chapter are designed to get you started. Play the games and drills in this chapter and your view of a tennis court will be changed forever.

German star Anke Huber appeared during the years when Steffi Graf claimed most of the limelight. Despite the challenge of being compared to Graf after her retirement, Huber rose to a career-high ranking of #4 in the world and always appeared to have a lot of fun doing it.

Description

This exercise is designed to help you focus while reducing any tendency you might have to become distracted while playing. You will need a group of friends or just some onlookers to play this game. The role of the onlookers couldn't be easier: While you play a tiebreaker, the onlookers should do everything in their power to distract you and your practice partner. While you're at it, rotate as many players into the action as possible to join in the fun. If you can focus in this environment, match play will be easy. It will even give you a taste of what it's like to be the foreign team playing the Davis Cup in front of an enthusiastic home team in South America!

Helpful Tip

Some onlookers may need encouragement to do their jobs properly. Tell them there are no rules of conduct apart from throwing anything onto the court. Screaming, yelling, booing, whistling, and generally distracting in any way possible are encouraged. They can even yell just as you are about to hit the ball.

Variation

Doubles can be played as an option to singles. Don't overlook this as a fun twist to a social club tournament.

Court to Court Over Fences

Description

This drill expands the size of the court as well as your perspective. Every tennis court has a fence—behind it, next to it, or in between courts. Let's assume that you and your partner will hit baseline-to-baseline groundstrokes, *but* you are on different courts. The two courts are positioned end to end, and each of you stands around the service line with your back to the net on your court. The balls must bounce once and land between the baseline and the back fence on each court. Therefore, your playing area will be about 42 feet long, because the normal distance between the baseline and the back fence is 21 feet. Rallying over a fence that is probably at least 10 feet high means you will be hitting a controlled, high-arcing ball. Try to cooperatively hit 20 balls in a row with topspin. This idea of hitting over fences can be expanded to dozens of variations for two or four players. Some of these are listed in the following variations, but you will be able to come up with many more on your own as well.

Helpful Tips

1. This exercise, when carefully executed, will be a great skill builder for topspin lobs.
2. Because more time than normal will lapse in between hits, you and your partner will tend to have less footwork than desired. Keep your feet "happy" by staying on your toes, and improvement is guaranteed.

Variations

1. Play a game over the same fence with balls landing within the other court's singles sidelines, but this time between the baseline and service line. Start with a bounce hit and play until one player reaches 11 points. You can either hit after one bounce or directly out of the air. Further options within this variation include a four-player drill with players alternating hits on each side, with the hitter sprinting forward to touch the adjoining fence after each shot.
2. Use courts that are laid out side by side to hit over the connecting fence. In this layout, turn the singles sidelines farthest away from the fence into your new baselines and play straight ahead on one side of the net. You can also play with two and four players, alternate or play doubles, play with serves or without, or play diagonally over a much longer area.
3. You can also use fences to practice lob volleys and ball control.

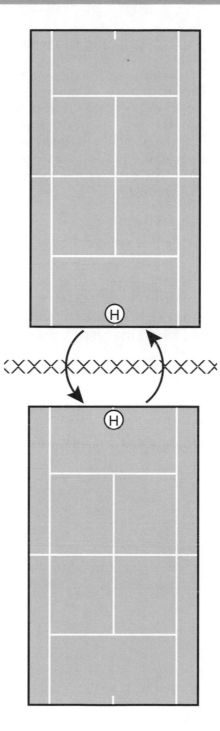

Walker

Description

Here's a simple yet effective way to help you focus, even in the midst of tremendous distractions. Hit back and forth with a practice partner baseline to baseline. Then, while you're hitting, a third player or coach walks back and forth across the court parallel to the net. Of course, the walker should time the move and keep alert to avoid getting hit. This exercise is a great way to get players to hit higher over the net. The result will be greater focus and improved consistency. Play out points from the baseline with no drop shots allowed, and players are not allowed to cross in front of the service line. The winner of each game keeps playing up to three games in a row, and the loser of each game rotates with the walker.

Helpful Tips

1. The walker can be on either side of the net but should walk directly alongside the net.
2. The walker should face the player hitting the ball just in case he needs to make a quick move to avoid getting hit.
3. This may seem obvious: Only do this drill with players who are mature enough not to make a joke of the game. Make sure they do not try to hit the walker.

Variations

1. You can let the walker hold a racket and swing it around to provide an even bigger distraction.
2. Require the walker to jog or sprint back and forth in erratic movements.

Shadow With the Sun

Description

This exercise is designed to fine-tune your skill at keeping the consistent open racket face needed for low volleys. The only limitation is that this drill must be performed around 10:00 A.M. or 4:00 P.M. on sunny days. Because tennis courts are almost always oriented north to south, you and a practice partner start by lining up along one of the service lines. One feeds and the other hits waist-high or lower volleys back to the feeder. The task for the volleyer is to freeze after hitting each low volley to observe the shadow created by the racket face. Ideally the shadow from the racket should not reveal any strings; it should be at approximately the same angle as the sun in the sky. Just the shadow of the racket edge should be seen. Once you gain consistency, you can increase the speed of the feed along with side-to-side or random hitting to lock in solid, low volleys. Rotate every 10 feeds.

Helpful Tips

1. The feeder will face directly into the sun, and the volleyer will have the sun shining at her back.
2. Keep in mind that the exact window of time will depend on the time of year. The idea is that the sun has to be 45 degrees off the horizon, or halfway between the horizon and directly overhead.

Variation

With more than one pair of players, create a competition. Have the feeders line up in one doubles alley on the same side of the net looking into the sun. The volleyers line up facing the feeders in the other alley with the sun on their backs. Feeders and volleyers must stay in their respective alleys; points are scored for each ball volleyed and caught by the feeder. The purpose of this drill is to reinforce correct volley technique. Therefore, after each volley, the hitter must freeze the racket face, look at the racket and the shadow, and say out loud, "Shadow with the sun." Play until one pair scores 10 points, and then rotate positions to play again.

360-Degree Slice

Description

This is a serving exercise that combines fun with learning a slice serve. Clinical studies show that aiming for the service box slows down the learning process because the server worries about whether the serve will land in the service box. Consequently, the server frequently tightens up; even though a loose and fluid motion is required, just the opposite occurs. Just serve without concern about where the ball lands. After every serve, move about 30 degrees until you complete a full circle on the baseline, concentrating on just slicing the ball. The balls will end up in all directions: to the next court, against the back fence, and so on. Simply observe which stance puts the ball into the service box, and use that position as a starting place for repetition drilling for your new slice serve. This exercise is a great drill that makes learning the slice serve more enjoyable.

Helpful Tips

1. If you are having trouble creating the proper spin, try to hit about 10 serves with the edge of your racket. This simple adjustment will take care of a lot of potential problems, including holding the racket with the wrong grip.

2. As mentioned earlier in this book, you can also kneel down (a right-hander kneels on the right knee) on one knee to get a better feel for how the wrist guides the racket head to hit a slice serve.

Variations

1. With two or more players, you can create a simple competition that will help everyone with their slice serves, but it will have nothing to do with putting the ball in the box. The priority is learning the slice serve, so rotate with the other players so that each of you hits one serve. The competition is to see which player can hit with the most spin regardless of where the ball bounces. Have all players vote on which one hit with the most spin, and the player who gets the most votes in each round is the winner. The scoring just adds a little fun because the main point of the exercise is to get more spin on your serve.

2. The follow-up to variation 1 is to count only those serves that go over the net; but again, it doesn't matter where the balls land.

3. Try the same drill of voting on which player creates the most spin; however, this time count only the serves that land in the correct service box.

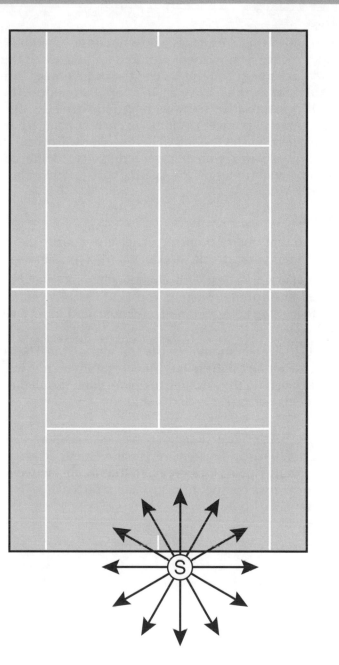

Chairs to Recover

Description

This drill uses props that are always near a tennis court—chairs—to encourage the proper recovery movement required for singles on the baseline. Set up two chairs, each about two feet behind the baseline and three feet to each side of the center baseline hash mark. On the opposite side of the net a partner, coach, or ball machine then feeds wide groundstrokes. After hitting each groundstroke, you will recover to sit in the correct chair (that is, diagonally opposite from where you hit the ball). This exercise will quickly teach you that when you hit crosscourt, your recovery distance to the correct chair is shorter. Hit 10 groundstrokes before rotating with another player or stopping to take a short break.

Helpful Tips

1. Make sure that chairs do not damage the court. And remember, the hotter the temperature, the greater the risk for damage.

2. This exercise works best with a ball machine because the frequency of the feeds can be predetermined. You want a steady yet random feed that allows the hitter enough time to recover and briefly sit down in the correct chair.

3. For safety, the feeds should be short enough so that the hitter is moving side to side along the baseline. You certainly do not want to push the hitter back behind the baseline to create even the slightest chance of a collision between a player and a chair.

Variation

You can add a point-scoring system to this movement drill by creating target areas. Simply award 1 point for every ball that lands crosscourt behind the service line. To create a competition, just keep track of how long it takes each player to accumulate 7 points.

Description

This exercise resembles a tug-of-war. Pair up with a partner and rally inside one of the doubles alleys. Each ball that lands in the alley scores 1 point. Make sure to call out loud your cumulative personal score after every point. Play until one player reaches 21 points. The initial bounce-hit feed must land in the alley but does not count as a point. If a ball misses the alley, keep it in play to try to score points. Play stops only if the ball lands in the net or cannot be returned. A bounce hit then starts a new rally.

Helpful Tips

1. If necessary, start hitting in front of the service lines to gain confidence and control.

2. You will have the tendency to stand flat-footed with any drill in a confined area. However, move as much as possible to get into a balanced hitting position when preparing to hit every shot.

Variations

1. If the alley proves to be too small an area for less experienced players, this drill also works well with any other designated area of the court.

2. You can handicap players of different levels by assigning a higher target number to the stronger player.

3. Using many pairs of players, you can easily adapt this drill to a combination of cooperative and competitive play by having each twosome work together as a team to accumulate points. Then, with many pairs starting at the same time on multiple courts, see which team is the first to reach 21 total balls in the alley. Every time that goal is reached, the players rotate clockwise in a circle to switch partners. The result is that each player will have a new partner and the entire group will start the exercise again. After each player drills with each of the other players, you can also track everyone's scores. This will reveal which player was the most consistent (that player with the most points) and which player was the least consistent.

Horizontal Drilling

Description

This horizontal (sideways) drill is an extension of drill 135, "Court to Court Over Fences." Like the other drill, this game creates a different perspective for players of all levels while it increases interest and fun. All that's needed are two side-by-side courts with either no divider fence or a three-foot fence between the courts. This drill breaks down the familiar barriers of a court, so you should feel more relaxed and have more fun while lengthening your strokes, because the court is slightly longer than normal.

Just as in a normal singles match, the balls can bounce once or be hit out of the air, and they must land in the backcourt area on each court behind the service lines and within the singles court. A bounce hit begins play; you and your drill partner face each other across the courts, each starting off in the farthest doubles alleys. The divider fence (where available) acts as the net. Cooperatively hit four balls back and forth, and then play out points with regular scoring. This drill reinforces the importance and necessity of keeping tennis practices visually stimulating.

Variations

1. Play doubles with the same rules. With four players on the court, poaching and faking are effective tactics.

2. Do variation 1 but alternate hits.

3. Play either singles or doubles, but no balls are allowed to bounce after the first four hits.

4. All of the variations can also be played on the diagonal across two courts. In this situation, the hitting area will be even longer, which will force players to extend their shots even more. This forced extension is particularly beneficial for players who tend to have short, choppy strokes.

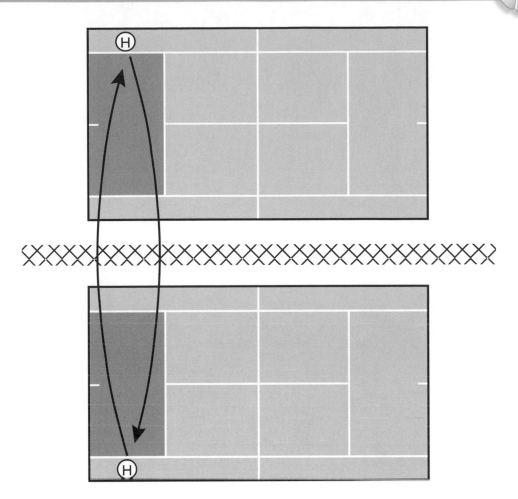

About the Author

Joe Dinoffer is a USPTA Master Professional with an extensive career in the tennis industry. He is founder and president of Oncourt Offcourt, Inc., and has conducted clinics and exhibitions in more than 50 countries. He has logged over 30,000 hours of instruction in English, Spanish, and German.

Dinoffer has written numerous articles for Tennis magazine, is a contributing editor for Tennis Industry magazine, and is the publisher of Coach Tennis America audio magazine. He is the author of 16 books, 20 videotapes, and more than 70 digital audiocassettes. Dinoffer is also a member of the Professional Tennis Registry and Intercollegiate Tennis Association. He is a frequent speaker at tennis conferences all over the world.

Dinoffer lives in Dallas, Texas, with his wife, Monika, and their daughter, Kalindi.

See the games on video!

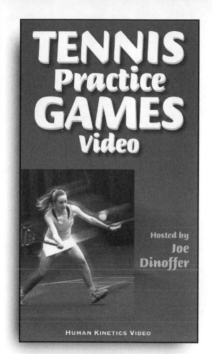

45-minute video
ISBN 0-7360-4690-9

Now that you've been introduced to the innovative game-based approach featured in *Tennis Practice Games*, it is time to take the action straight to the court. The *Tennis Practice Games Video* presents clear, visual demonstrations of 42 of the most creative and complex games featured in the book. You will see exactly how the games and variations play out with slow-motion and expert commentary. Make every trip to the practice court more productive and rewarding with the *Tennis Practice Games Video*.

To place your order, U.S. customers call
TOLL FREE 1-800-747-4457.

Customers outside the U.S. should place orders using the appropriate telephone number/address shown in the front of this book.

HUMAN KINETICS
The Premier Publisher for Sports & Fitness
P.O. Box 5076, Champaign, IL 61825-5076
www.HumanKinetics.com

2335